Yoshie Moriki

Low Fertility and Local Values through the Lens of Demographic Anthropology

Living Arrangements of the Elderly in Thailand
and Sexuality and Reproduction in Japan

春風社
shumpusha
publishing

LOW FERTILITY AND LOCAL VALUES
THROUGH THE LENS OF DEMOGRAPHIC ANTHROPOLOGY

Living Arrangements of the Elderly in Thailand and
Sexuality and Reproduction in Japan

Yoshie Moriki

Low Fertility and Local Values through the Lens of Demographic Anthropology aims to show how the population structures in a society and the values held by local people interact with each other. The macro-demographic context influences the daily life experiences of people, while the behaviors of people, conditioned by cultural norms produce and reproduce demographic patterns. Two case studies on the living arrangements of older people in Bangkok and sexuality and reproduction in Japan clearly illustrate the two-way relationship between population dynamics and people's behaviors. The first study on the determinants of living arrangements in Bangkok shows that the number of never-married children is a significant factor influencing co-residence with an adult child in old age. What is more, the key factor for co-residence is to have at least one child who recognizes the concept of *bun khun,* which is the expectation that children will pay back their debts to their parents by taking care of them in old age. Results from the second study on sexual and reproductive behaviors among single males in Japan reveal a separation between men's sexual desires and intimate feelings for a specific partner. It also shows the preference given to solo sexuality, or masturbation, in Japan. Analyses from the two case studies show how macro population dynamics and local value systems are strongly intertwined. In addition, the book also explores innovative ways to combine both qualitative and quantitative methods to deal with population issues while also paying attention to ethnographic contexts.

Yoshie Moriki is a Professor at the International Christian University in Tokyo, Japan. She obtained her Ph.D. in Anthropology and Demography from Pennsylvania State University in 2007. Her research area is cultural anthropology, with a specialization in demography. Her current research focuses on intimacy and reproductive issues. She has conducted research in Thailand, Laos, and Japan.

CONTENTS

ACKNOWLEDGMENTS……10

INTRODUCTION……13

    Aims of this Book……15

    A Contribution to Demographic Anthropology……17

Chapter 1 THE SOCIAL CONTEXTS OF LOW FERTILITY……23

    The Case of Thailand: Population Aging and Elderly Care……25

    The Case of Japan: Sexuality and Reproduction……33

Chapter 2 METHODOLOGICAL CHALLENGES: CAPTURING LARGE POPULATIONS, QUANTITATIVELY AND QUALITATIVELY......41

Data Collection in Bangkok: Statistical Considerations and Ethnographic Approach......43

Data Collection in Tokyo and Other Parts of Japan: Exploring Alternative Methods......69

Chapter 3 LIVING ARRANGEMENTS OF ELDERLY PEOPLE IN BANGKOK: THE IMPORTANCE OF HAVING A *BUN KHUN* -MINDED CHILD......77

Traditional Old-age Co-residence 79

Determinants of Living Arrangements: Quantitative Results......83

Ethnographic Insights: Qualitative Results......100

Conclusions......117

Chapter 4 SEXUAL AND REPRODUCTIVE BEHAVIOR AMONG SINGLE MALES IN JAPAN……121

Meaning of Sexual Activities: Social Sexuality and Solo Sexuality……124

Dating Relationships and Reproductive Future with the Girlfriend……137

Conclusions……142

Chapter 5 CONCLUSIONS……145

BIBLIOGRAPHY……151

INDEX……163

LIST OF TABLES

1.1 Key demographic estimates and projections, 1970 to 2040 27

1.2 Total fertility rates and life expectancies at birth, 1965–1970 to 2045–2050 28

2.1 Comparisons of distribution patterns of demographic variables, corrected for cluster sampling design effects (95 percent Confidence Intervals in parentheses) 58

3.1 Weighted percentage distribution of the living arrangements of the elderly people in Bangkok, all cases and those with an adult child (unweighted n in parentheses) 84

3.2 Weighted percentage for elderly people co-residing with an adult child, by marital status of co-residing children (unweighted *n* in parentheses) 85

3.3 Weighted means and percentages of the characteristics of surviving adult children (S.E. in parentheses) 87

3.4 Weighted percentages by marital status and age category (unweighted *n* in parentheses) 87

3.5 Weighted percentages for place of residence, by marital status of the children (unweighted *n* in parentheses) 88

3.6 Weighted means and percentages of predictive variables used in the logistic regression of co-residence with an adult child, among elderly people with an adult child 92

3.7 Logistic regression of co-residence with an adult child, among elderly people with an adult child 94

ACKNOWLEDGMENTS

During my childhood, several people jokingly said to me, "You will write a book someday." They seemed to have liked my writes for fun or school assignments. I never took their words seriously nor had the urge to write one. But this book still came out of my academic path, and I am happy that the stories that had accumulated over the years are finally out there for readers. It shouldn't have taken so long, but at the same time, I feel that the time was needed for the book to be ready.

This book would never have been possible on my own. I am very grateful for all of the support I have received, technically, emotionally, and financially. To begin with, if I had not received various scholarships and grants, including the Rotary Foundation Academic-Year Ambassadorial Scholarship Award, Mellon International Demography Training Fellowship, and a Doctoral Research Improvement Grant from the National Science Foundation (NSF), the whole endeavor would not have started. I am hugely indebted to my Ph.D. advisor, Patricia Johnson, for her support throughout my graduate study. I am also thankful to other committee members James Wood, Gordon de Yong, and Mark Hayward, for showing me professionalism as researchers and warmth as educators. Meeting these professors was one of the lucky things that happened in my life. My project in Thailand was generously supported by Pramote Prasartkul at the Institute for Population and Social Research (IPSR), Mahidol University; the Office of Population Technical Assistance Team (OPTA); and various research assistants who patiently helped me. Furthermore, my involvement in cultural anthropology started when I took courses with Kouichiro Uno at my university in Tokyo. It is his intellectual input that cultivated my curiosity as a learner.

I would also like to acknowledge many colleagues, friends, and institutions in Japan. Naohiro Ogawa, the former director of Nihon University's Population Research Institute (NUPRI), and Rikiya Matsukura, a colleague at the same institute, made my career in Japan more exciting by introducing me to the topic of sexless marriages. I am grateful to have been a member of NUPRI from the very beginning of my work life after my doctoral degree. Manabu Akagawa and Shoko Konishi from the University of Tokyo have been powerful motivators in their pursuit of sexuality and reproductive issues. I am also grateful to the Japan Society for the Promotion of Science (JSPS) for providing project funding to investigate male sexual and reproductive behaviors in Japan (grand-in-aid for scientific research C, 21K12508). I also would like to thank Shumpusha Publishing for encouraging me to publish this book. Finally, my thanks go to Jenny Yamamoto, who edited this book and has followed its development from Bangkok to the present.

Last but not least, I would like to thank my family. Without them, this book would not have been finished. The first son who was born during the fieldwork in Bangkok turned 20, and the second son who was born in Tokyo in the middle of organizing an international conference on low fertility and reproductive health became his late teens. I am grateful to my family, whose enduring support has nurtured both my career and my journey as a mother.

Yoshie Moriki
Koganei, Tokyo
Summer 2024

INTRODUCTION

Aims of this Book

This book discusses the relationships between population dynamics and the values held by local people in society, focusing on two specific topics from Thailand and Japan. The first case from Thailand investigates the living arrangements of the elderly in Bangkok. The second case from Japan examines reproduction and sexuality. Demographically speaking, both societies are struggling with the consequences of sustained level of low fertility. The first aim of this book is to show how population dynamics are affecting the lives of people in each society, particularly in the context of low fertility.

Population dynamics, on the other hand, are influenced by the value systems embedded in society. Drawing on ethnographic information, the second aim of this book is to reveal the underlying structures and conditions in the two societies. The importance of having children who recognize the concept of *bun khun* (a Thai concept that obligates children to take care of aged parents) is highlighted as a critical factor for achieving old-age co-residence in Thailand. Meanwhile, the Japanese case explores heterosexual sexuality and intimacy, shedding light on the separation between sexual desires and intimate feelings held in a committed relationship. It is shown to be often incompatible for men to hold sexual desires and warm feelings towards their partner resulting in infrequent sexual activity within a committed relationship. Population dynamics are produced and reproduced in the cultural context that conditions the behaviors of the people living in it. Through the case studies presented in this book, the workings and meanings of these cultural contexts will be discussed.

Finally, the third aim of this book is to contribute to methodological approaches in the field of demographic anthropology. The two case studies presented here take a holistic approach using both quantitative and qualitative data. For Thailand, the quantitative analyses are based on over 1,000 cases sampled from the entire Bangkok Metropolis. As part of the author's dissertation research conducted in 2003, a local interview team and the author collected representative data using a questionnaire schedule that was designed to follow the lives of respondents in a flexible manner. Qualitative information was gathered through in-depth life history interviews with both elderly parents and their co-resident children.[1]

The data for Japan were collected in 2022 through a total of eight focus group discussions. Focus groups are a good way to gather qualitative information in a less interventionist manner. Beyond the general advantages of focus group discussion techniques, two methodological points make this data unique. First, the participants of the discussions

---

[1] Some parts of Chapters 1, 2, and 3 have been written for my doctoral dissertation and updated as needed for this book.

were recruited from a pool of willing respondents who had already participated in a survey about male reproduction in 2020. Second, the focus groups were held online using Zoom,[2] which helped promote active discussions on potentially sensitive topics regarding sexuality.

Thus, the analyses and discussions presented in this book build on over 20 years of various data collection activities that combined both quantitative and qualitative methods. Moreover, the Thai case study provides details of the fieldwork process in order to share practical ideas on how to collect ethnographically oriented data in a large city such as Bangkok. Some of the ethical issues that emerged during the data collection process are also evaluated here.

A Contribution to Demographic Anthropology

This book is intended to serve as a contribution to the field of demographic anthropology. Demographic anthropology is a subfield of anthropology that specializes in topics related to population. Since both anthropology and demography are intensely interested in the daily activities of people, these two fields inherently have many qualities in

---

2   Zoom is a video conference platform provided by Zoom Video Communications (https://www.zoo.us).

common. However, there are surprisingly few academic works published under the category of demographic anthropology. The scarcity may come from methodological complications of collecting and analyzing both large-scale population-based survey data and ethnographically motivated text-based data under a single research theme. In this respect, Kertzer and Fricke (1997: 1) describe the demography-anthropology relationship as "tortured and passionate." This book comes out of the struggles and joys of trying to make sense of social issues from both a survey-based demographic viewpoint and an ethnographically-minded anthropological perspective.

Looking back at the author's academic journey, this exciting trial of combining demography and anthropology was initiated during her university days in Japan. As a senior student majoring in area studies, she was interested in the concept of being old in Thailand and wrote a thesis on the meaning of old age by interviewing elderly Thai people living in the province of Kanchanaburi. Then at graduate school in the United States, she majored in cultural anthropology and later joined the demography program offered by the Population Research Institute at the university. That was the formal beginning of a long-term commitment to the field of demographic anthropology.

For her doctoral research, the author decided to investigate the issue of population aging because it was already a serious demographic problem in Japan and was expected to become an emerging issue in

Thailand. It was her first attempt to empirically study a specific issue from both macro (demographic) and micro (ethnographic) perspectives. In the theoretical framework of demography, people's behaviors can be summarized in terms of fertility, mortality, and migration. These activities are expressed as demographic indicators, such as the Total Fertility Rates and Infant Mortality Rates. Thus, demographers examine these indicators to gain a macro-level understanding of changes in people's behaviors. On the other hand, from a micro ethnographic viewpoint, peoples' behaviors need to be observed in their daily lives in the local context. The ideas and thoughts of local people need to be sought in the value systems embedded in each society.

What is intriguing is the interaction between macro population dynamics and micro value systems. People adjust and change their behaviors depending on macro population dynamics, while population dynamics, in turn, are affected by peoples' behaviors shaped by local value systems. The macro and micro are interrelated, producing a specific social phenomenon. The inter-play of population dynamics and value systems has become an important focus of the author's research.

Academic work cannot be done without data. Sources of data and ways to obtain them are important. Without reliable data, researchers cannot conduct fair analyses, develop interpretations, and draw conclusions. The problem is that data do not come into the hands of a researcher by itself. Someone needs to give it to them. For an anthropologist, the people who give you data, or rather, the people who teach you how a system works in a particular society, are your informants. Anthropologists are serious about building trusting relationships with these informants. An informant is not just a person who responds to your questions.

On the other hand, for a demographer, the people who give you data are your respondents. Because of the nature of population studies, demographic work usually requires a large number of cases to perform statistical analyses. Therefore, demographers typically work with second-hand data, gathered by a third party, such as censuses and nationally representative surveys. Direct and involved relationships with respondents are not something that usually preoccupies demographers. What makes the field of demographic anthropology unique is that it allows the researcher to engage in the challenging tasks of combining different methodologies and handling the ethical issues that arise from different data collection styles. This book is the result of such an attempt.

The book is organized into five chapters. Chapter 1 describes two types of low fertility issues observed in Thailand and Japan. Both countries are facing social problems arising from sustained low fertility rates. The chapter briefly provides background information to understand the particular social phenomena that are explained in later chapters. Chapter 2 is devoted to methodological challenges in obtaining quantitative and qualitative data in a single study, particularly with large populations.

Chapter 3 investigates the living arrangements of the elderly in Bangkok, with a focus on the significance of the concept of *bun khun* and *bun khun*-minded children. Chapter 4 examines the sexual and reproductive behaviors of single males in Japan by highlighting the separation between men's sexual desires and intimate feelings in a committed relationship, as well as the priority given to solo sexuality, masturbation. Finally, Chapter 5 restates the challenges of low-fertility societies and discusses some underlying ethnographic issues in Thailand and Japan.

Chapter 1

THE SOCIAL CONTEXTS OF LOW FERTILITY

This chapter presents an overview of the demographic backgrounds of Thailand and Japan. Both societies face certain challenges of aged societies which arise from rapid fertility reduction and continuous low fertility rates. The two case studies focus on issues that are significant for demographic dynamics in societies with low levels of fertility. The first case about Thailand looks at the impacts of low fertility on family structures. The second case about Japan relates to inactive sexual activity in a committed relationship, which is a suspected cause of low fertility. For both cases, it is important to understand how people experience the social contexts of low fertility.

The Case of Thailand: Population Aging and Elderly Care

Fertility reduction and population aging

This section discusses the demographic background of Thailand, focusing on the country's drastic fertility reduction and resulting aging of the population. It also examines the emerging demographic trend of never-married individuals in Thailand, particularly in Bangkok. Thailand is one of the few countries in Asia that achieved a more than 60 percent reduction in the total fertility rate (expected number of live births to a woman in her lifetime) over 25 years, starting in the 1970s (Gubhaju and Moriki-Durand 2003). As a consequence of this marked shift towards low fertility, an inevitable growth in the numbers and proportion of the elderly population has been expected.

The demographic indicators in Table 1.1 show that the population of Thailand has become increasingly older from the 1970s towards the early 2000s when the fieldwork for this case study was originally conducted. The number of older people (defined here as people aged 60 years and older) has more than tripled in the 30 years from 1970 to 2000, and by 2040, the over-60 population is expected to be more than three times the figure for 2000. The percentage of people aged 60 years and older was under five percent in 1970 but gradually increased to over nine percent in 2000. In contrast, the younger population (younger than 25 years old) shrank from about 64 percent to 44 percent between 1970 and 2000, and is expected to further decrease to 30 percent by 2040.

This rapid growth in the proportion of older people in Thailand has largely resulted from a sharp decline in fertility. As shown in Table 1.2, the total fertility rate (TFR) decreased from six children per woman in the period 1965–1970, to three in the period 1980–1985, and has since been below the replacement level for over 20 years. It is projected to remain at this level over the next 50 years. The successful implementation of the National Family Planning Program that started in the early 1970s is the prime contributor to this drastic fertility decline (Rosenfield et al. 1982). Given the latent desire of couples to control the number of children, the program worked well in providing the needed contraceptive services

Table 1.1 Key demographic estimates and projections, 1970 to 2040

	1970	1980	1990	2000	2025	2040
Population aged 60 and older (thousands)	1,777	2,409	3,442	5,714	13,946	18,666
Percentage aged over 60	4.9	5.2	6.3	9.3	19.2	24.9
Percentage aged under 25	63.7	61.0	53.4	43.5	32.7	29.6
Percentage aged over 80	0.3	0.3	0.4	0.7	2.1	4.3

Source: United Nations (2005). World Population Prospects: The 2004 Revision (Medium Variant), Vol. I: Comprehensive Tables.

(Robinson and Rachapaetayakom 1993). As a result, contraceptive use became highly prevalent within just ten years of the beginning of the program; as early as 1981, 58 percent of married women were using some method of contraception, while 79 percent reported having ever used contraception. The prevalence rate was high (52 percent currently using and 74 percent ever used), even among women with less than elementary school education living in rural areas (Kamnuansilpa et al. 1982).

A major reduction in the mortality rate also occurred during the same period, as indicated by the increasing life expectancy at birth. Table 1.2 shows that life expectancy at birth in Thailand steadily increased from 59.1 years to 64.9 years between the periods 1965–1970 to 1980–1985, and then to 69.0 years for the period 1995–2000. It is expected to continue to increase over the next 50 years, and is projected to reach

Table 1.2 Total fertility rates and life expectancies at birth, 1965–1970 to 2045–2050

Year	1965–1970	1980–1985	1995–2000	2010–2015	2020–2025	2045–2050
Total fertility rate (children per woman)	6.0	3.1	2.0	1.9	1.9	1.9
Life expectancy at birth (years)	59.1	64.9	69.0	73.1	75.5	79.1

Source: United Nations (2005). World Population Prospects: The 2004 Revision (Medium Variant), Vol. I: Comprehensive Tables.

almost 80 years in 2045–2050.

These population dynamics provide the demographic context for Chapter 3, which examines elderly people's living arrangements in Bangkok. People aged 60 years and older at the time the original fieldwork was conducted in 2003 were born in or before 1943, when fertility rates were still high. The majority of these elderly people produced many children during the pre-fertility transition period, before the introduction of the National Family Planning Programs in the 1970s, by which time even the youngest elderly cohort was already at least age 26. As Jones (1993) suggests, people who are born during the last phase of high fertility are predicted to face the most serious aging problems, because they belong to a large population cohort but were likely to have had significantly lower reproduction during the post-fertility transition period. In this regard, the most severe aging problems in Thailand have been projected to occur roughly between 2030 and 2045.

As was anticipated in the early 2000s, Thai society has been rapidly aging over the past 20 years. According to the National Statistical Office of Thailand, the percentage of people aged 60 years and over increased from 9.4 percent in 2002 to 19.6 percent in 2021 (NSO 2022). Thailand's TFR has remained low during these years: 1.57 in 2002, 1.55 in 2013, and 1.33 in 2021. At the same time, life expectancy at birth increased from 72.9 years in 2002 to 77.1 years in 2013, and further to 78.7 years in 2021 (United Nations, Department of Economic and Social Affairs, Population Division 2019a). It is apparent that Thailand has become one of the leading aged societies in Asia.

In response to this rapid rate of aging, many researchers have expressed warnings. One of the biggest worries is about financial support for the elderly population. According to Sujatha and Reddy (2012), though the Thai government has been trying to reform its social security system, the system is immature and does not meet the needs of the elderly population.[1] From an economic viewpoint, Thailand can be said to have entered the aging stage too quickly without achieving a strong economy. In addition, Kumagai (2019) points out that Thai companies are struggling with labor shortages. Although companies are trying to adapt to the

---

[1] Currently, about 30 percent of the labor force in Thailand is covered by a pension plan (Sujatha and Reddy 2012).

problem by introducing automated production systems, the future is not looking promising. A professor at the Institute for Population and Social Research, Mahidol University, argues that given the aged population, the Thai government needs to promote more healthcare and social welfare spending to support its elderly population. She also worries that as a consequence of population aging, intergenerational tensions over social resources can happen in the near future (Punpuing 2023).

Implications of population aging: Erosion of family care?

With the rapid reduction in the fertility level and the expected decline in the younger population, there has been growing interest in the future of the old-age care systems in Asian countries, including in Thailand where the family has traditionally taken the main role in supporting elderly people. A major issue involves a commonly expressed worry about the erosion of extended families and the expected decline in the welfare of the elderly. For example, Mason et al. (2002) anticipate the traditional reliance on family support for old age in Asian countries will deteriorate and warn that families may not be able to shoulder the financial burden of an aging society. Similarly, Martin (1988) predicts a decline in the extent to which elderly people live with their children, as was the case in Japan.

Aware of the potential erosion of the familial care system, governments in Asian countries have responded primarily by emphasizing the importance of existing family support systems. The Thai government also places strong emphasis on the preservation of the extended family care system and associated social values of respect for elderly people. For example, the Second National Long-Term Plan for Older Persons, endorsed in 2002, stresses the individual responsibility to prepare for old age and the role of families to support individuals. In the plan, government and public resources are mentioned only as the last means for those who fail to secure familial support (Jitapunkul et al. 2002). Thus, although the Thai government realizes the reality of an aging society, it continues to recognize the family as the major provider of old-age support in Thailand.

Another issue in the picture is the rapidly rising rate of non-marriage, particularly among females in Bangkok. According to Jones (2004), the percentage of never-married females aged 40 to 44 and 45 to 49 reached 9.3 percent and 8.0 percent, respectively, while 7.8 percent of males aged 40 to 44 and 5.1 percent of males aged 45 to 49, were still single in 2000. The corresponding figures in 1970 were 3.9 percent and 3.0 percent for females and 3.1 percent and 2.3 percent for males. Furthermore, in 2000, 19.9 percent of Bangkok females aged 40 to 44 and 17.3 percent of those aged 45 to 49 were still single. The never-married proportions for Bangkok males aged 40 to 44 and 45 to 49 were 15.4 percent and 10.9 percent, respectively (Jones 2004). It is remarkable that in Bangkok, about one out of six females who have passed their presumed reproductive period has never been married. In fact, Jones

(2005) suggests that the level of non-marriage among Bangkok females aged 45 to 49 is exceptionally high compared with the same age group in other Asian cities, such as Metro Manila (9.0 percent), Hong Kong (5.9 percent) and Singapore (13.5 percent for Chinese, 7.5 percent for Malays). In addition, Williams et al. (2006) have observed that the growth in never-married proportions is increasingly greater for men, suggesting a possibility of a marriage squeeze for lowly educated men. In 2010, the percentage of never-married men aged 40 to 44 and 45 to 49 reached about 15 percent and 11 percent, respectively, while those for women were 11 percent and 10 percent (calculated by the author using United Nations 2019b).

From the viewpoint of long-term population structure, non-marriage is a worrisome issue. As Jones (1998) points out, a decrease in the proportion of currently married women contributes to a further reduction in total fertility rates, and prevailing non-marriage will likely ensure the persistence of below-replacement fertility. However, having more single people may turn out to be a benefit for Thai society, at least in the short term, since never-married people can be available as resources to aging parents. If single people continue to live in the parental house, the expected impact of fewer children may be mitigated by the continuing presence of children living at home.

Chapter 1 THE SOCIAL CONTEXTS OF LOW FERTILITY

The Case of Japan: Sexuality and Reproduction

Sexlessness in Japanese society

In recent years, the sexlessness phenomenon has attracted keen social and academic interest in Japan. In particular, the reproductive behaviors of so-called sexless couples have been studied together with the problems of sustained low fertility rates and the resulting contraction of the population. Over the last 10 years, researchers have speculated that sexlessness, particularly sexless marriages, is a hidden cause of low fertility in Japan (Moriki et al. 2015). According to several national surveys, the percentage of "sexless" people[2] is as high as about half of all married people. For example, two rounds of the National Survey of Work and Family that cover males and females aged 20–59 years old reported that 45 percent (2007) and 44 percent (2010) of married respondents had sexual intercourse with the spouse less than once a month (Moriki and Matsukura 2022). Other surveys by Japan Family Planning Association that target people aged 16 to 49 years old further suggest that the percentage of sexlessness among married people has

---

2   In 1994, the Japan Society of Sexual Science defined a couple as being "sexless" "if, despite the absence of unusual circumstances, there has been no consensual intercourse or other sexual contact between them for a month or longer and it is expected that such a state will further persist over a longer period of time" (Abe 2004: 18).

been increasing from 31.9 percent in 2004, 34.6 percent in 2006, 36.5 percent in 2008, 40.8 percent in 2010, 41.3 percent in 2012, and 44.6 percent in 2014 (Kitamura 2015). Although it is not easy to compare the level of sexlessness between the two surveys due to differences in survey specifications,[3] it is undeniable that Japanese people have passive attitudes toward marital sexual activities.

Some studies discuss reasons for inactive sexual behavior. Genda and Kawakami (2006) found that long working hours are a cause of sexlessness. Kitamura (2009) argues that besides tiredness from work, having sex with the spouse itself is not counted too highly as indicated by such responses as "no particular reason after a birth" and "(having sex is) too tiring." In addition, Moriki et al. (2015) show that not only the long working hours of the husband but also having a child less than three years old is a significant determinant of sexless marriages. Besides statistical results, their study includes qualitative data obtained from focus group discussions. Words of participants reveal that Japanese couples become a family by going through events like marriage and/or childbirth, the process of which reduces the importance of sexual activities as a couple in the daily lives of Japanese people.

It has long been pointed out that joint activities as a couple have

---

[3] It needs to be noted that the surveys by the Japan Family Planning Association do not specify the partner of the reported sexual intercourse.

not taken root in Japanese society. For example, Ato (2000) cites the immaturity of the dating culture in Japan as one of the factors behind the increase in non-marriage. Looking at data showing the rise in the age of first sexual experience and the fall in the proportion of unmarried people who have experiences, Sato (2019) claims that since the 2000s, detachment from sex has been occurring not only among married people, but among unmarried people as well. Furthermore, Yuyama and Nimura, who are not academic researchers but have written and spoken on issues about sexuality in the media for many years, published a book in 2016 called *The Japanese May Stop Having Sex*. In the book, the authors explain that due to a lack of sexual education and the spread of pornography, having sex with respect and intimacy towards each other is getting to be a rare event in Japan (Yuyama and Nimura 2016). From these various indications, it is reasonable to say that sexual behavior as an activity of couples is now weakening.

Pregnancy intentions and frequencies of sexual intercourses

Accumulated findings suggest that marital sexual activities are not regarded highly in Japanese society, and sexless couples themselves do not necessarily see sexlessness as an urgent problem. From the viewpoint of reproduction, however, the frequency of unprotected sexual intercourse is one of the direct determinants of fecundity, and (having sexual intercourse) once a week is a frequency that is often mentioned as sufficient frequency, which would let women in prime reproductive age conceive within one year (see Bongaarts and Potter 1983; Wood 1994). So, it is understandable that the lower frequency of sexual intercourse is associated with a longer waiting time for conception, and because of the low frequency, a couple can fall into "infertility" even though there is no specific medical cause (Konishi et al. 2018).

Special attention should be drawn here to the frequency of sexual intercourse for women in their 30s and 40s. Since the average age of first marriage for Japanese women is close to 30 and the percentage of out-of-wedlock births remains very low,[4] the sexual behaviors of women in these age categories are important for fertility estimation. According to the previously mentioned survey "Work and Family" (2010), as much as 37 percent and 44 percent of married women in their 30s and 40s were sexless. In addition, women who reported having sexual intercourse with their spouse once a week or more were as low as 17 percent (30s) and 10 percent (40s) (Moriki and Matsukura 2022). This result is consistent with Sato's (2008) hypothesis that the low frequency of intercourse may be one of the factors contributing to the downward trend in the marital fertility rate, given the low rate of contraceptive usage and the continuously

---

4   The average age of first marriage for women in 2020 was 29.4 years, and out-of-wedlock births accounted for 2.4 percent of all births (National Institute of Population and Social Security Research 2022).

declining abortion rate.

Indeed, what is intriguing is that surveys suggest that the frequency of sexual intercourse, even among people who explicitly plan pregnancy, is low. The National Survey of Work and Family includes data on the frequency of sexual intercourse of respondents who want to have (one or more) children. Among such respondents, those who had sex at least once a week were not very high (37 percent of respondents in their 20s, 20 percent of respondents in their 30s, and 16 percent of respondents in their 40s). The percentages of sexless respondents were also 22 percent (20s), 37 percent (30s), and 50 percent (40s). Furthermore, Konishi and Tamaki conducted an online survey of women aged 20–44 titled "Biodemography Project" in 2014 to examine the time it takes to conceive. According to their results, among married women who wanted children immediately, only 24 percent had intercourse with a partner at least once a week, while 38 percent had intercourse with a partner 1–3 times a month (Konishi and Tamaki 2016).

It should be noted that while the country suffers from low fertility, having children is still a strong social value in Japan. According to the results of the National Fertility Survey carried out by the National Institute of Population and Social Security, the proportion of the never-married in Japan who felt that marriage had certain benefits stood at around 60 percent for men between 1987 and 2015 and fluctuated between 70 and close to 80 percent for women. Regarding what respondents considered to be concrete benefits of being married, the percentage of those who chose the answer "having children and family" was as high as 31.1 percent among males and 39.4 percent among females in 2021.[5] Another popular opinion "marriage gives one peace of mind" started falling in 1997 and was chosen by 33.8 percent of men and 25.3 percent of women in 2021 (National Institute of Population and Social Security Research 2023). In other words, most never-married Japanese seem to perceive that being able to obtain children and family is one of the greatest necessities and advantages of marriage.

Values related to mothering and preference for Kawanoji co-sleeping

Many studies argue about the strength of the influence of "mothering" as a structural feature of Japanese society. For example, Goldstein-Gidoni and Lebra showed "childcentrism" to be the life purpose of Japanese mothers (Goldstein-Gidoni 2012; Lebra 1984). Tsuya (2004) pointed out that strong familial norms are embedded in Japanese social systems, and society expects women to fulfill their roles as wives and mothers, making it difficult for them to balance childcare and work. There is also the opinion that due to the robust mechanism of valuing the family, common law marriage and out-of-wedlock births

---

[5] The percentage was even higher for the previous survey in 2015 (35.8 percent for males and 49.8 percent for females).

are not functioning as substitutes for the drop in the rate of marriage (Sato 2008). We can thus see that because the sociocultural value system emphasizes having and raising children, the family centering on the mother and her children continues to be the keystone of Japanese society.

The child-centered family system enforces the internalization of motherhood. Lebra (1984) states that in this child-centered family, the needs and demands of the child are given the highest priority, and parents, especially mothers, tend to be seen as being there for the child. Furthermore, Moriki's paper reports the narrative of a female focus group participant in her 20s who lost interest in sexual intercourse after the birth of her child "because she is a mother" and has been sexless for several years since the pregnancy and birth of her first child (Moriki 2012). As in this case, the strong internalization of the cultural norm that "because I am a mother... (I do not engage in couple activities such as sexual intercourse)" is thought to have led to a preference for being the mother of a child over sexual life.

Furthermore, physical contact with children is openly emphasized in Japanese society. In Japan, *skinship* (literally meaning physical contact, especially between a mother and her child) is expressed by such common practices as parent-child co-bathing and co-sleeping, which are supposed to strengthen the emotional bonds between parents and children (Shand 1985). In particular, parent-child co-sleeping is widely observed and valued in Japan. Studies have explained that the preference for co-sleeping is attributable to the Japanese cultural emphasis on harmony and connectedness. Small (1999) suggests that Japanese parents are trying to instill a sense of dependence, an important quality in the harmonious Japanese society, in children through co-sleeping arrangements. Research by Moriki (2012; 2017) also argues, based on several rounds of focus group discussions, that a distinctive sleeping arrangement called *kawanoji* co-sleeping (where children sleep between parents in the shape of the Chinese character for river, *kawa* 川) is a manifestation of cultural values that emphasize happiness as a family. As exemplified by the parent-child co-sleeping practice, the physical intimacy between parents and children and the physical "un-intimacy" between couples are functionally connected in the concept of the Japanese family. It can be said that the growing sexual distance between the spouses is a natural consequence of practices to maintain the family, and sexless marriages can be considered a part of the process of forming families.

Chapter 2

METHODOLOGICAL CHALLENGES: CAPTURING LARGE POPULATIONS, QUANTITATIVELY AND QUALITATIVELY

By describing the process of data collection for the two case studies, this chapter aims to provide practical methodological ideas for those who are interested in conducting fieldwork with large populations, especially in an urban setting. In particular, those who would like to collect both large-scale statistically sound quantitative data and ethnographically oriented qualitative data may find it useful. Ethical issues involved in ethnographic research are also visited. The chapter attempts to re-evaluate some of the ethical issues that were not resolved earlier.

Data Collection in Bangkok: Statistical Considerations and Ethnographic Approach

Sampling issues

As Askew (1994) has pointed out, anthropological studies equipped with traditional participant observation techniques often have methodological difficulties in dealing with large populations. On the other hand, studies that use survey techniques face the challenge of balancing the collection of large-scale data on the one hand, and understanding the views of local people on the other. Recognizing these methodological dilemmas, the study attempted to examine the whole city by collecting representative data without losing sight of localized views.

One of the devices used towards this end was the methodological focus on the census block. The Bangkok Metropolis is administratively divided into districts called *khet*, and within the administrative framework of the *khet*, the census block is used by the National Statistical Office of Thailand (NSO) to conduct surveys. A census block is the primary sampling unit, organized to contain about 100 to 200 households.

To collect representative data from the whole of the Bangkok Metropolis, census blocks were used as the primary sampling unit (PSU) for the project. The specifications and methods for the sampling were:

> 1) Observation unit: an elderly person (aged 60 and over) residing in the Bangkok Metropolis. An elderly person was counted as "residing" at a house if he/she was considered to be regularly living at the house (i.e., eating and sleeping there on a daily basis) by him/herself or other members of the household,[1] regardless of the official housing registration.
>
> 2) Target population: elderly people currently residing in a household in the Bangkok Metropolis.
>
> 3) Sampling unit: census block. NSO helped randomly select one census block from each administrative district in the Bangkok

---

[1] Based on the pilot study and local understanding, a household is defined as a group of people who usually live together and share the same basic house utilities, such as electricity, water, and gas.

Metropolis.

4) Sampling frame: the official list of all census blocks for each district in Bangkok. The sampling design of the project is one-stage cluster sampling, in which the census blocks in each district are the clusters.

5) Household listings: based on the maps of the selected census blocks, the project team members created the household listings. The household listing identified: a) the number and location of households in each census block; b) the total number of elderly persons in each household, if any; and c) the sex of the elderly person(s).

Although cluster sampling is often criticized for having lower statistical precision (Sudman 1976), for this study, the clusters worked effectively as a kind of ethnographic space. Since a census block covers between 100 to 200 households, it is a reasonably sized area to walk without a car, grasp a basic sense of the area, get to know the residents of the block, and obtain information important to the area and the people living there. It would have been more difficult to secure this local information had prospective interviewees been randomly located throughout the Bangkok Metropolis. The information gained through observations and casual conversations also proved important for judging the adequacy of the statistical results and for interpreting them.

Roads in the central Bangkok in the 2020s

Area surveys, mapping, and household listing

The area surveys involved confirming the exact locations of the selected census blocks, which were spread over the Bangkok Metropolis. The area surveys were an important step for the project for several reasons. First, the maps provided by the NSO were quite rough, often lacking names of the streets and rivers that were necessary for finding the area. For each area, the author and the research team walked around the locality, noting essential features such as the names of major markets, the numbers of *sois* (streets branching off of major streets), and the names of *muu baan* (villages or gated communities), and added them to the original maps. When there was a disparity between the map and reality, we updated the map as well. This was necessary more often than one would expect, partly because of the speed of physical changes in Bangkok. Despite being time-consuming, visiting all blocks, one by one, provided a sense of the characteristics of each block and the people living there.

The mapping and listing stage not only identified prospective interviewees but was also a valuable preparation for implementing the project. First, this stage introduced the interview team members to people living in the target census blocks, so that the residents could recognize the interviewers during the actual interviews at a later stage and feel more comfortable with their presence. Because Bangkok is a big city and people are wary of strangers, being known in the area was an important step in gaining access to houses for interviews. Second, it was also a good opportunity for the interviewers to get to know their allocated census blocks. In fact, they quickly grasped the characteristics of each area and were able to provide useful local information, including rumors, demolition plans in a community, the origin of a community, the daily life patterns in a block, etc. The author was able to compare notes with the interviewers and learn more about each area from them.

Interviewer training

Before starting the survey, the interview team went through intensive survey training with the author and Thai managers. The main goals of the training sessions were first, to train the 10 Thai interviewers to be competent in conducting an interview session independently, and second, to train them to reduce response biases resulting from the interviewers. The training helped to standardize the way interviewers asked questions and recorded answers, especially for those questions that could be interpreted differently, depending on the way they were asked.

Along with the core training sessions, a series of informal sessions was also provided to equip the interviewers to deal with practical issues associated with fieldwork. The Thai managers gave advice on how to dress and behave and emphasized the importance of conveying a non-threatening presence to reduce possible fears about strangers. The project supplied two T-shirts with the NGO's logo, a bag, and a name tag for each interviewer to use during work time, so that people in the study areas could know who they were and feel more comfortable with them. The managers also instructed them on appropriate ways to explain why the interviewers were in the study block, using a letter of introduction from the author's host institution in Thailand.

Interview with questionnaire

The training session was immediately followed by the interview stage, which lasted approximately three months. The prescribed course of an interview session was: to first locate the house of an eligible elderly person using the household listing and neighborhood map; approach the prospective interviewee and show the letter of introduction from the host institution; explain the informed consent form and obtain their consent; conduct the interview; and end the interview session with words of thanks and a small gift as a token of appreciation. The interviewers repeated this process from the first to the last eligible person listed on the household listings of each census block. On a good day, an interviewer could conduct up to five interviews, but on average, one interviewer could complete only three interviews per day. The actual interview session (i.e., from the time after the introduction, to before the post-interview chatting time) took about one hour on average. However, on some occasions the interviewer spent hours at the house of the interviewee, drinking water, eating food, and listening to her/his stories, which the author encouraged the interviewers to do when they had the chance.

The manager and the author paid careful attention to the allocation of census blocks to the different pairs of interviewers. Every effort was made to assign the same interviewers to the same blocks in the household listing stage, so that the interviewers were already familiar with the location, composition, and ambiance of the block. As Bangkok was infamous for its traffic congestion, knowing exactly how to get to the block was very important; if they got lost or caught in bad traffic, not only time and money would be wasted, but the enthusiasm of the interviewers for the project itself could also diminish. By this point, each interviewer had befriended several reference people in each block, an especially welcoming elderly person, a helpful *yaam* (guardsman), or an official or unofficial community leader. These people helped the interviewers gain access to prospective interviewees when the interviewers returned to the block for an interview.

Using the knowledge from the household listing stage, the team tried to find the most convenient time for an interview for each census block. Since each block had its own characteristics and lifestyles, it was possible to make an educated guess about the probable times when the prospective interviewees were likely to be free to participate in interviews. For example, in a low-income area, elderly people were typically at home during the day, watching their grandchildren or working in the neighborhood for a small income, and it was usually fine to visit them on a weekday. On the other hand, in a relatively wealthy housing estate, elderly people were often not home during the day, visiting elsewhere. Even if they were at home, they would most likely not come to the door as they tended to be afraid of strangers. They also may have been instructed by their children not to open their doors. In these cases, the interviewers needed to visit them over the weekend, when their children were around.

Challenges faced

The interview team encountered several challenges in approaching households and collecting interview data. A seemingly trivial but ultimately serious threat to interview visits was presented by both stray and house watchdogs. Stray dogs were abundant in Bangkok, especially outside of central Bangkok districts, where they often roam in packs. Some packs are comprised of more than twenty dogs. When these dogs were wandering around the *sois*, the interviewers understandably felt nervous, and they needed to take precautions to avoid being attacked. Sometimes, the presence of dogs slowed the pace of interview visits for the day. Moreover, house watchdogs, either tied up or running freely inside the gates of a household, were also potential obstacles to interview visits. Relatively wealthy households typically had several watchdogs that started to bark as soon as they spotted the interviewers. Because these dogs were big and strong, there were several incidents in which elderly women were willing to talk with the interviewers but could not control their dogs, so the interviews needed to be rescheduled. Fortunately, the team did not experience a serious attack by a dog, but the presence of dogs was something that always affected the interviewers.

The hardest challenge the team faced was accessing and obtaining data from Chinese-Thai people.[2] The author was initially alerted to the potential problem when a pair of distressed interviewers called from a block with predominantly Chinese-Thai residents to inform her that they could obtain data from only a few people in the block. This was confirmed by the very low response rate, less than 20 percent, of the first round of interviews. After holding a team meeting, we realized that there were several factors that made it difficult for Chinese-Thai elderly people to participate in the interviews. First, many Chinese-Thai elderly people, especially those who are first-generation immigrants, can speak only one Chinese dialect, and even those who speak Thai may not be fully fluent. Second, as most of them are involved in trading businesses, there is a strong reluctance to waste time in a non-money-making activity.[3]

Accordingly, the author looked for a Chinese speaker to become

---

2   The word "Chinese-Thai" here refers to people who regard themselves as being of Chinese origin, regardless of their nationality status, Chinese speaking ability, Chinese cultural competencies, or what generation of immigrant they are.

3   Coughlin (1960) describes the overseas Chinese as "very flexible people whose main concern is self-interest" (p. 193), and who value being "materialistic, concerned principally with the acquisition of wealth as an end in itself or as a means to social position" (p. 197).

Stray dogs in Bangkok

an interpreter for the team and was introduced to a middle-aged Chinese-Thai housewife. She had grown up speaking *Teochiu,* one of the major Chinese dialects spoken in Bangkok, at home, and had learned Thai at school. *Phii* Lek (older sister Lek), joined the team and began accompanying the interviewers as an interpreter.[4] Her presence helped open the doors of Chinese-Thai people, and people chatted with her more casually than with the other interviewers. As a result, the response rate in the Chinese-Thai areas greatly improved. Her "Chinese" phenotype with whiter skin, and her casual conversation in *Teochiu*, helped make the Chinese-Thai people feel more comfortable. As a second-generation person from a Chinese-Thai family and someone who still practices Chinese traditions in her daily life, elderly people felt that she was "one of them" and consequently were more open to being interviewed for the project.

Another strategy was to assign a Chinese-Thai interviewer from the interviewer group to cover predominantly Chinese-Thai areas. One of the interviewers identified herself as being Chinese-Thai and was also seen by others as belonging to this group. In her early thirties and with more experience than other interviewers, she was helpful in giving the team tips on the basic nature of Chinese people. According to this interviewer,

---

4   All names used for people and places in this chapter are pseudonyms.

Chinese people are afraid of people they are not familiar with, and will not take action unless they see tangible benefits (such as financial gain) in doing so. She advised interviewers to talk quickly with Chinese-Thai people because they are very time-conscious. If they are bored or feel that they are wasting time, they will terminate the interview. Even though she could not speak any Chinese dialects, her identity as a Chinese-Thai who lived in a shophouse in the area known as Chinatown, contributed to good response rates from Chinese-Thai people.

To conclude, in spite of the challenges and problems, the data collection went smoothly, and 1,125 interviews were completed. The collected data reasonably reflected the results of the census 2000 (Table 2.1). According to the post-interview questionnaires answered by the interviewers, what they liked about working on the project were: 1) feeling the generosity of people; 2) learning from the experiences of elderly people; 3) getting to meet many people from different social categories and knowing more about different areas of Bangkok; and 4) spending time with elderly people who sometimes needed someone to talk to.

In-depth interviews

In addition to the general survey, the research design included in-depth interviews with five pairs of elderly parents and married children; another five pairs of elderly parents and non-married children; and an additional five non-co-residing elderly people. The main concern about

Table 2.1 Comparisons of distribution patterns of demographic variables, corrected for cluster sampling design effects
(95 percent Confidence Intervals in parentheses)

Item	Category	Census 2000 (5,671 cases)	Collected Data (1,125 cases)
Mean age	In years	68.6 (68.4–68.8)	70.2 (69.8–70.6)
Sex	Male	44.8% (43.5–46.1)	36.7% (34.2–39.3)
	Female	55.2% (53.9–56.5)	63.3% (60.7–65.8)
	Sex ratio	0.77	0.59
Marital status	Never–married	5.4% (4.9–6.1)	5.4% (3.5–8.2)
	Married	67.7% (66.5–68.9)	57.7% (51.5–63.7)
	Widowed	22.5% (21.5–23.7)	29.6% (25.5–34.2)
	Divorced	4.0% (3.5–4.5)	7.3% (5.4–9.7)
	Unknown	0.3% (0.2–0.5)	—
Religion	Buddhism	94.8% (94.2–95.4)	97.0% (92.7–98.8)
	Islam	3.8% (3.3–4.3)	2.3% (0.7–7.3)
	Other	1.4% (1.1–1.7)	0.7% (0.3–1.6)
Nationality	Thai	94.0% (93.4–94.6)	97.1% (95.3–98.2)
	Chinese	5.3% (4.7–5.9)	2.8% (1.7–4.6)
	Other	0.7% (0.5–0.9)	0.2% (0.0–0.7)
Educational level (highest attained)	No education	22.6% (21.6–23.7)	12.4% (9.9–15.3)
	Elementary	51.6% (50.3–52.9)	58.8% (54.4–63.1)
	High school	12.0% (11.2–12.9)	15.1% (12.6–17.8)
	Above high school	9.8% (9.0–10.6)	13.8% (10.4–18.1)
	Unknown	4.0% (3.5–4.5)	0.4% (0.1–1.0)

the identification process of potential interviewees was to ensure that people from a variety of social categories were included. The specific criteria used for selection were: 1) socio-economic status of both elderly parents and their children (high, middle, and low); 2) type of living arrangements (co-residence or non-co-residence); and 3) sex and marital status of co-residing child (ever-married or never-married).

After the potential interviewees had been selected and the survey data entry into a file was almost completed, the author and an interviewer from the team, Noi, began the interviewing stage, with the author as the main interviewer and Noi as the interview assistant. All interviews were conducted in Thai, except in three cases where the interviewees could speak fluent English and preferred to have interviews in English. Noi sometimes added words to the author's sentences or restated what she had said when her Thai was not clear enough for the interviewees to understand well (by this time, Noi was good at understanding the author's often imperfect Thai). When interviewees were not fluent in central Thai but fluent in *isaan* (a northeastern dialect related to Lao), Noi took the leading role and talked to them in *isaan* as he was a native of this area. For interviews with a Chinese-Thai elderly woman, the aforementioned *phii* Lek accompanied us so that the elderly person could talk with us in *Teochiu* when needed.

On a typical interview day, the author and Noi would meet in the residential area of the target interviewee and then visit the household together. In all cases, the elderly interviewees remembered that they had been interviewed by a young interviewer a couple of months previously (for the survey) and were therefore not particularly surprised to see us. The elderly people whom Noi had interviewed before remembered his face right away and welcomed us before we said anything. The course of the conversation was semi-structured, based on an interview guide that listed topics and questions. The responses of interviewees, however, were not restricted and they were free to add anything they thought was important. Even though we did not set any time restrictions, a typical interview could take one to three hours, depending on the situation. The prepared topics were usually comfortably covered within this time, and the interviewees often showed with subtle gestures that they had finished. Given the style of interviewing and the daily schedule generally followed by people in Bangkok, two hours seemed to be the length of time people felt comfortable spending with a "familiar stranger."

Interviewers as ethnographic informants

One of the major methodological goals of this project was to find ways to deal with the whole of Bangkok without losing the views of its local residents. One means toward this end was to employ a group of local interviewers, train them well, and, when appropriate, include their insights on the questionnaire schedule and answer categories. However, beyond fulfilling these initial expectations, the interviewers in effect functioned as a group of additional ethnographic informants to teach the author what "Thainess" was and to help the author make sense of what she was dealing with. She learned how Thai society worked in a broader framework, beyond the research questions, through their behaviors, comments, and reactions. For example, it was through them that the author started to understand the meaning of a key Thai concept, *nam jai* (generosity), which is said to be the center of Thai personal relations.

The interviewers were helpful as providers of emic information as Thais, yet they also retained their objectivity as trained outsiders studying a group to which they did not belong, the elderly. This worked well as it provided the author with localized information in each block and gave her clues to better understand what was really happening in the field. For instance, they told her about a plan to demolish a whole block for the construction of a new highway. The people living in that block would have no other choice but to be evicted from their residences without meaningful compensation when the time came. In contrast to the author's surprise, the interviewers did not seem to be surprised by the government's conduct. The author later realized that this kind of eviction was common in Bangkok, especially among poor residents. She started to understand why people were often being *chui chui* (showing an impassive attitude towards something that could be challenging and adverse); they were used to a life of unreasonable incidents and a life without choices.

Overall, the fieldwork was a process of growing together as a team.

Recognizing that the author saw herself as a student of Thai culture, the interviewers also made efforts to improve themselves as interviewers. Although most of the interviewers were already experienced, they still needed to gain confidence in conducting this type of questionnaire as part of a team, knocking on the doors of strangers in a city like Bangkok. They also had to find ways of dealing with the author on a daily basis, as they realized that she was going to be with them instead of disappearing into an office at a university. Looking back now, one of the most difficult parts of the fieldwork was to guide the interviewers toward the research goals as the project leader, and at the same time be guided by them as a novice in their culture.

What the author learned from the intensive contact with the interviewers was the importance of including the "right" kind of interviewers on the team, beyond a simple qualification like "college student" or "previous experience as an interviewer." These qualifications may help anticipate a person's ability to absorb the training sessions properly and adequately digest the information provided. However, the author found that even though good training was necessary to collect reliable data, there was a limit to what training could provide. For example, an interviewer's maturity, life experiences, and background or upbringing, are qualities beyond the reach of interviewer training.[5] Yet,

---

5   For example, Noi, one of the male interviewers, was a very talented interviewer. Unlike other interviewers, he was especially competent in dealing with people

these elements turned out to be extremely important, particularly for securing good response rates and for conducting quality interviews based on a naturally flowing conversation. More importantly, if one expects to spend a major part of fieldwork with these interviewers and to indirectly learn about their culture through their behaviors, it is sensible to include these qualities when selecting interviewers.

Besides the day-to-day methodological challenges discussed earlier, one of the most unexpected and psychologically intricate issues encountered during the fieldwork was the difficulty of human resource management. The fundamental issue that the author was forced to handle was that of being a *nai jaan* (employer) in Thai society, where the concept of patron-client relationships is pervasive. While the author had read about patron-client relationships, considered by ethnographers as the fundamental building block of Thai social relations, the author did not initially realize that this concept also applied to her, and that she was expected to play the role of patron.

In patron-client relationships, people occupy a position in the social hierarchy based on their level of accumulated *bun* (merit) and are

---

from higher social categories. The author could not understand the reason for his skills, as his background seemed similar to that of other interviewers. One week before the end of the project, he told the author that he was the son of a minor wife of a powerful man in his native province. He grew up knowing the privilege of power, even though he never actually employed it.

expected to behave accordingly. A person who stands higher in the social order gives out benefits from the greater resources he/she has to people whose position is lower, in exchange for the services they provide (Hanks 1975). Historically, the patron-client relationship has its roots in the scarcity of labor in Thailand and the necessity of effectively organizing it for political and economic purposes. The patron-client relationship in its original form consisted of *nai* (masters; princes and nobles) and *phrai* (mostly peasants) who were required to register under a *nai*, as part of a class system in which the *nai* provided protection and assistance, while the *phrai* paid respect to the *nai*, conformed to the *nai*'s requests, and rendered services and gifts (Rabibhadana 1975). The patron-client relationship in this form no longer exists, but the basic structure is still an important mechanism for Thai social relationships (Heim et al. 1983).

Once the author saw herself as a patron, the words and behaviors of Thai people started to make sense, like the pieces of a puzzle falling into place. For example, a Thai professor who acted as a mentor repeatedly said that showing *nam jai* (generosity) to the interviewers is important to make them happy and to keep the project going. In fact, this professor, and many other professors whom the author met in the field as her superiors, never failed to show generosity of different kinds.

To play the role of patron, the author initiated several practices that aimed to increase the level of protection and assistance to the interviewers. One of the benefits the author managed to provide from her limited capacity as a patron was flexibility in the work schedule. Contrary to her expectations, the interviewers did not want to take regular days off during the project, except for an occasional day off for running errands. This was important as the interviewers lived on the wages the project paid them and could not afford to take many days off. As a result, they worked more days per month than the estimated 20 working days that were based on two days off per week. The author gradually understood that the pre-defined wage was just a basic condition of employment. A trusting relationship, whereby the interviewers felt that they would receive additional unspecified benefits, needed to be established if the author wanted to keep them for a long period of time. As the author developed patron-like behaviors, the interviewers became more dependable and showed a greater willingness to perform extra duties for the project and for her.

Fieldwork and ethical issues: Revisiting my fieldwork

The fieldwork described here was conducted in 2003–2004. About 20 years have passed since that time; during those years, the author became a professional demographic anthropologist, teaching and conducting research at a university in Tokyo. To be honest, for a long time, it was difficult to look back at what the author had achieved and had not achieved in the field, because of the intensity of the field experience. With time, however, it gradually became easier to revisit the experience to evaluate issues that could not be totally resolved before. For example, it gave the author time to reflect on issues such as fairness in researcher-informant relations during data collection. Growing public interest in the application of ethnographic methods in recent years also motivated the author to re-examine the delicate issues she encountered during the fieldwork.

One unforgettable incident that happened during the data collection process was when she encountered a Chinese-Thai elderly woman living in a shophouse in a predominantly Chinese area. The author asked her to participate in the interview. She replied, "If I help you by answering your questions, what do I get? As a result of giving my time to you, you will have my answers and you will become a professor. Then, what do I get?" The author was totally shocked by her questions. The author had brought a little gift as a token of appreciation, but it was obvious that she did not mean that. The author cannot remember exactly how she responded, but this incident bothered her for a long time after the end of the fieldwork. The elderly woman was right: what was the author trying to do for respondents? The author had innocently entered the daily lives of local people in the name of research, but was she aware of the potential impact of these encounters?

This elderly woman made her realize the power of the ethnographic approach to literally "touch" the lives of subjects. The author still thinks that there is no single answer to her question. However, with time, the author is more and more sure of the (negative) impacts of ethnographic methods on research subjects. Because the ethnographic approach is so powerful, its users need to know that they are not just accessing respondents to obtain data. Our interactions can potentially affect them in one way or another, and we need to honestly confront these possible impacts. Hopefully, the impacts are positive ones, but unfortunately, this may not always be the case.

Second, when the author was conducting in-depth life history interviews, a few elderly people started to cry in the middle of the interview. The interview topic was the history of living arrangements, with details of the informants' children coming in and out of their households. Informants usually had several living children, and they would explain which children lived together with them, at what time, and why these children had left home or had not left home. Such information was needed to account for the history of living arrangements leading into their old age. The research plan had been reviewed and approved by the Institutional Review Board at the author's university, and no potential problems had been pointed out. She therefore felt very awkward and sorry when the elderly informants began to cry, but did not know what to do. At that time, all she could do was listen to what they needed to say. For example, one elderly woman explained that her eldest son had been arrested for selling drugs, the second son had died in a traffic accident, her elder daughter had met a man and disappeared, and the youngest child was living with her but could not find a job to make a living. Another informant, an elderly man living in a poor neighborhood, shouted at the author with frustration, saying, "I am living like this. You know? What kind of child would like to live with me?" All the author wanted to find out was the history of their living arrangements, but that inquiry also touched upon the past failures and successes of their lives. Now, with the experience of having raised children of her own, the author can tell how painful those questions may have been to some of the informants.

In retrospect, the author even feels ashamed and regrets asking such potentially insensitive questions. It is not clear, however, what she could have done differently back then. The author provided an informed consent form pointing out their rights, including not having to answer any questions they did not feel comfortable with, and the right to withdraw from the interview at any time. She was careful to protect them as much as possible, but the fundamental issue was not that. Anthropologists are equipped with ethnographic methods that "touch" the lives of our subjects. Although it is not easy to provide a clear solution to this issue, it should be stressed that ethnographic methods have an impact on people, and those who use them are responsible for how they are used. There can be various practical ways of taking responsibility, depending on the situation and capacities of each researcher. What is fundamentally crucial is to take such ethical issues seriously before, during, and after the fieldwork.

Data Collection in Tokyo and Other Parts of Japan: Exploring Alternative Methods

Use of internet panels in academic research

One of the methodological difficulties of a project in demographic anthropology is to collect both large-scale population-based data and ethnographically oriented qualitative data. The following discussion is about a recent attempt to collect such data on the sexual behaviors of Japanese males. Chapter 4 presents the qualitative results from this attempt,[6] while methodological issues in producing data are highlighted in this section.

The study described here first started as a subproject of "Interdisciplinary Investigation on the Technology, the Environment, and Fertility (IITEF)" led by Dr. Shoko Konishi from the University of Tokyo, funded by the Japan Society for the Promotion of Science (JSPS) Topic-Setting Program to Advance Cutting-Edge Humanities and Social Sciences Research, Global Initiatives Program. IITEF aims to examine the impacts of technology and the environment on fertility trends in Japan. The author was in charge of one of the subprojects under IITEF which is named "Technological Innovations and Variability in Sexual Behavior."

A unique feature of this subproject of IITEF is the employment

---

6 Please refer to the article (Konishi et al. 2022a) for the quantitative results from the survey data discussed here.

of two web-based questionnaire surveys. One survey is a retrospective questionnaire focusing on the history of respondents' sexual behavior, including masturbation, over 20 years. The other survey is a cross-sectional questionnaire that aims to obtain information about the sexual activities of married and single Japanese males with a focus on the types of sexual partners. Both surveys were conducted online in September 2020 (Konishi et al. 2022a). Interestingly, even though internet panels and online data collection were chosen as a way to manage the research during the COVID-19 pandemic, online data collection turned out to be a preferred method for this research which involved intimate questions.

For the project, we contracted Rakuten Insight, Inc. which has more than two million registered Rakuten members across Japan. The eligibility criteria for this survey were to be male, aged 20–54 years, and living in Japan. There were 661,604 eligible men in the Rakuten Panel. From the eligible members of the Rakuten Panel, screening questions (whether to consent to participate in the survey, the prefecture of residence, age, and marital status) were sent to 150,559 randomly selected people. So, in a sense, our respondents can be regarded as those who were randomly selected from a population called "Rakuten Country." Out of those who received screening questions, 12,811 people answered, and 9,713 completed the main survey (Konishi et al. 2022b).[7]

---

[7] According to the results of the 2020 census, the male population between the ages of 20–54 was 27,437,317 (Konishi et al. 2022b).

Increasing numbers of academic studies employ internet panels like Rakuten Panel to recruit survey participants. There are, however, recurrent questions and doubts about the representativeness of data obtained from an internet panel, compared with data from a standard stratified random sampling method. Recognizing such concerns, we set the final number of respondents by five-year age category and eight geographic regions were to be relative to the corresponding proportion of the male population in Japan in the 2015 National Census. Nonetheless, since we were also curious about the reliability of internet panels for academic use, we investigated the representativeness of our respondents. According to the analyses (Konishi et al. 2022b), the percentage of men with lower education (junior and high school graduates) is less in our data than that of the 2020 National Census (24 percent vs 38 percent). In addition, the percentage of never-married men is lower in our data.

Having recognized potential sources of bias in data obtained through an internet panel, the author suggests that the use of internet panels and online data collection should receive more serious attention in academic research. In particular, when a research topic is sensitive, accessing and collecting data from potential respondents online has clear advantages. First, respondents can be recruited on an individual basis via a PC or a smartphone with much less risk of family members, colleagues, or friends knowing about the survey participation. Answering questionnaires online can also secure more privacy than the traditional paper-based method.

Second, when the internet-based method is used, potential respondents are given several chances to think about the survey before deciding to participate. That is, the potential respondents first willingly register with a panel, and then when a particular research topic is presented, they are given detailed information about survey participation before signing an informed consent. It is undeniable that such voluntary participation is a source of bias in research. However, consented participation is crucial for obtaining earnest answers, especially when it comes to a sensitive topic like sexual behavior. Third, online data collection has the advantage of reaching out to a large number of people in a short period at a relatively low cost. This point is important not only for economizing the research budget but also for collecting data in a concise period to avoid changes in a social environment that can affect respondents' behavior.

Conducting focus group discussions using Zoom

Another unique point about this research activity is the development of the project from survey data collection to focus group discussions. As explained earlier, the idea originally started as a subproject of IITEF in 2019. Given the research findings from the 2019 project, the author obtained further funding from the Japan Society for the Promotion of Science (JSPS) in 2021. The study entitled "Where the Sperm Goes and the Male's Intentions: Qualitative Analyses of Sexual and Reproductive Behaviors in Japan" aimed to shed light on qualitative aspects of sexual behaviors of Japanese males. Two researchers from the sexual behavior segment of IITEF joined the study as co-investigators. As the analyses of survey data progressed, we came to think that exploring the meaning of quantitative results is needed to gain a fuller understanding of reproduction and sexuality in Japan.

For this qualitative study, we decided to employ the focus group discussion (FGD) technique as the major data collection method. FGDs are a kind of collective conversation or group interview on a particular topic, which are now recognized as a powerful data collection method (Rodriguez et al. 2011). FGDs also have a good reputation for enhancing group dynamism by grouping people who share similar characteristics or experiences and by creating a comforting atmosphere to encourage discussions without pressure or coercion (Fallon and Brown 2002). The author had used FGDs several times in the past for studies related to sexlessness in Japan, and knew that, indeed, participants are surprisingly open about expressing their thoughts even about sensitive topics once a session starts. So FGDs were chosen as the preferred method for this qualitative study about Japanese male sexuality.

A definite advantage when preparing for the FGDs for this study was the fact that the large-scale survey data collection had already been completed. Among the survey participants, about 60 percent indicated that they were willing to participate in further studies. This made it easier to recruit focus group participants from the survey respondents. One of the challenges of conducting focus group discussions is forming groups of people with appropriate common characteristics. As indicated in a study by Delva et al. (2010), it is more desirable to create a group of people with common traits that are relevant to the research question. For example, for the sexless issues, it was ideal to create a group of people with similar frequency of sexual intercourse to enhance active discussions. It is often not easy, however, to know the needed information to create a group beforehand. In this sense, having a pool of respondents for whom basic information is available was a benefit.

Furthermore, we decided to conduct the focus group discussions online using Zoom. The decision was partly due to the restrictions related to COVID-19, but more due to the advantages of online communication for this type of research. Luckily, the spread of online tools during the pandemic made it an optimal time to hold discussion sessions online. One of the greatest advantages of using Zoom is the fact that it became possible to recruit participants from any part of Japan. So, it was possible to strategically recruit participants to form groups, based on more research-oriented criteria such as people who have "both a specific partner as well as a casual sex friend," regardless of geographical location. Another advantage is the privacy that online communication itself provides. Participants can talk more freely because they are talking to strangers online, not face-to-face, about a specific and intimate topic. They were instructed to use a pseudonym for the session and not to mention personal information during the talk. We assured them that no information that could be linked to personal information would be revealed, and participants were also asked to promise not to talk about the contents of a session after it ended.[8]

As explained above, the data used in Chapter 4 were collected in innovative ways. Collecting data for statistical analyses and qualitative analyses in one project is challenging, and connecting the two types of data collection methods is another challenge. However, making use of new technology, it is becoming more feasible to achieve reasonable results. Of course, there are a number of issues to be further worked on. For example, conducting focus group discussions online is convenient for gathering people from different geographical areas. As a downside, however, the participants must have certain technological capabilities (a PC or mobile phone and internet connection) as well as a private environment for discussions. Having the needed equipment does not seem to be a big problem, but securing a private place for intimate discussions turned out to be more difficult for some people.

---

8   Researchers, including the author, had no individually identifying information about the participants. Rakuten Insight took care of the payment (in the form of Rakuten Points), using the last four digits of the phone numbers.

Chapter 3

LIVING ARRANGEMENTS OF ELDERLY PEOPLE IN BANGKOK: THE IMPORTANCE OF HAVING A *BUN KHUN*-MINDED CHILD

Thailand has undergone rapid fertility reduction, and the declining number of children is expected to have negative impacts on the traditional old-age care system that has been organized around co-residence. Based on first-hand data, collected through fieldwork conducted in 2003–2004, this chapter examines those factors that determine old-age living arrangements in Bangkok, Thailand. As discussed in detail in the previous chapter, the fieldwork was organized so that the data captured both macro population issues as well as micro ethnographic contexts. As a result, over 1,000 cases of survey responses and 28 cases of taped in-depth interviews were gathered for analysis.

Traditional Old-age Co-residence

Many studies agree that the predominant form of old-age living arrangements in Thailand has traditionally been co-residence with a married child. In ethnographies on rural Thai social systems, conducted mainly in villages located in north and northeast Thailand, Thai elderly people are usually found in extended households, surrounded by the family of a married daughter (Cowgill 1968; 1972). Following a common post-marital residence practice, sons often live with their wives' families after marriage, while daughters remain at their parents' house for a short period of time until they can arrange their own households.

As children gradually marry or move out to their own households, the youngest married daughter tends to be the one who permanently lives with and cares for the aging parents and eventually inherits the parental house (De Young 1955; Podhisita 1994). Based on these ethnographic accounts, matrilocality has been posited as the traditional post-marital Thai preference.[1]

Another important aspect of Thai households is that they repeat a basic developmental cycle over the course of marital development. In this cycle, after the initial period of co-residence with parents, a newly married couple moves out to establish a nuclear household when they are ready, or often as the result of the marriages of younger siblings. Following the births of children, their growth, and eventual marriages, the newly formed nuclear family develops into a stem family, in which one of the married children continues to live with the aging couple (Foster 1978; 1984). If a household follows the expected cycle, the parents have opportunities to live with different sets of married children during the period when children are getting married and leaving home. Then, finally, the aged parents can enjoy the benefits of co-residence with one married child who

---

[1] A closer examination of post-marital residence patterns by ethnicity and locality, however, reveals a more complex picture. Patterns differ between Thais and Chinese-Thais; the latter tend to prefer patrilocality (Chamratrithirong et al. 1988).

stays permanently at the parental house.

The underlying ideology that supports this household developmental cycle is the children's obligations to support their aged parents. According to Rabibhadana (1984), the most important concept that defines Thai family relations is the reciprocal ties organized around the idea of *bun khun*, which is described as "the favor or benefit, which has been bestowed on one, and for which one is obligated to do something in return." This concept obliges children to pay back debts to their parents for giving birth to them and bringing them up, but these debts are described as impossible to repay entirely. Van Esterick (1996) also discusses the Thai word *liang* (supporting, caring for, or tending) in connection with the reciprocal relationship between mothers and children. A mother is seen as having expended time, energy, and money in providing her breast milk to her children. The cost of breast milk (or canned milk in the modern context), recognized as *kha nam nom* (milk price), is the amount of debt that the children owe to the mother. The strong sense of indebtedness to parents, apparent in these concepts, comes from the Buddhist belief that being born as a human being is itself the great benefit that a child has already received from the parents, since "only man can learn of the Buddha's teachings and have a chance to reach Nirvana" (Rabibhadana 1984: 5).

The feeling of indebtedness, and the underlying Buddhist teachings, further provide a conceptual basis that prescribes different ways boys and girls can show their gratitude to their parents. In elaborating the reciprocal relationship between parents and children, Rabibhadana (1984) explains that a boy can pay back significant debt by becoming a monk, an act reserved for men.[2] Because people believe that having a boy ordained generates sizable merit for his parents, ordination provides a good opportunity for reciprocation for boys. On the other hand, girls, who do not have such a chance, have to repay their debt by supporting their parents in daily life by physically taking care of them and/or financially providing for them.

Another important premise of the developmental cycle of households and associated traditional co-residence with a married child in old age is that people follow the expected life cycle, involving marriages and childrearing. The developmental cycle of households would not "develop" if children did not marry; the household would continue as a nuclear family with increasingly aging children and elderly parents. However, given the increasing prevalence of non-marriage, it is important to re-examine the developmental process of households and to pay more attention to the marital status of co-residing children.

---

2   Ordination, especially for a short period of time (typically for about three months), is traditionally seen as a prerequisite for marriage, giving males the opportunity to repay the debts to their parents before entering a new family relationship (Pramualratana et al. 1984).

Determinants of Living Arrangements: Quantitative Results

Results of Cross-tabulations: Dominance of "Co-residence"

Table 3.1 shows the distributions of living arrangements of the elderly people in this study.[3] The types of living arrangements are divided into four mutually exclusive categories: 1) co-residence with an adult child (households consisting of elderly person(s) and an adult child, with or without a spouse, minor children, or others); 2) co-residence with a spouse (households consisting of elderly person(s) and a spouse without an adult child, with or without minor children or others); 3) co-residence with others only (households consisting of elderly person(s) and others without an adult child or a spouse, with or without minor children); and 4) living alone (households consisting of an elderly person without a child, a spouse, or others). Among all elderly respondents, 78 percent co-reside with an adult child. This figure compares with Wongsith and Siriboon

---

3 All analyses in this chapter were performed using Statistical Package for Social Science Version 13.
The overall response rate for this project is:
Response rate = $\frac{1,125}{1,125 + 433 + 236 + 35} = \frac{1,125}{1,829} = .62$; where the number of completed interviews =1,125, number of refusals=433, number of no-contacts=236, number of respondents incapable of answering = 35.
The analyses were weighted for cluster sampling effects and under-representation of Chinese-Thai people.

(1999), who state that 75.4 percent of the elderly in Bangkok (those who live in one sampled census block) co-reside with a child. Among those elderly with at least one adult child, the co-residing proportion is even higher at nearly 85 percent, confirming the high prevalence of co-residence.

Table 3.1 Weighted percentage distribution of the living arrangements of the elderly people in Bangkok, all cases and those with an adult child (unweighted *n* in parentheses)

Living arrangement (Living with)	All cases		Elderly with an adult child	
Adult child	78.3	(881)	84.4	(881)
Spouse	9	(101)	8.7	(90)
Others	9.4	(110)	4.8	(49)
Alone	3.2	(33)	2.1	(21)
Total	100	(1,125)	100	(1041)

Children include own children, stepchildren, and adopted children. There were a total of 29 stepchildren and 22 adopted children. Others include parents, siblings, grandchildren, children-in-law, other relatives, friends, and live-in house helpers.

Next, a closer examination of co-residence patterns suggests that the dominance of "co-residence" with an adult child may not be a simple continuation of the traditional model of old-age co-residence. In past studies, Thai elderly people have been portrayed as living in an extended

Table 3.2 Weighted percentage for elderly peeople co-residing with an adult child, by marital status of co-residing children (unweighted n in parentheses)

Living with		
Married child only	37.8	(319)
Both married & divorced child	1.4	(15)
Both married & never-married child	21.0	(186)
Never-married child only	35.4	(321)
Both never-married & divorced child	1.5	(12)
Divorced child only	3.0	(28)
Total	100	(881)

household with the family of one of their married children, and these extended families have been viewed as a security net for the elderly. However, Table 3.2 reveals that the involvement of married children in co-residence is not as high as might be expected. Even among the elderly who have at least one adult child and co-reside with one of them, only 60.2 percent of co-residence involves a married child. On the other hand, as much as 56.4 percent of co-residence is with a never-married child, including 35.4 percent of co-residence with only a never-married child. Thus, even though "co-residence" with an adult child is often treated as the typical traditional living arrangement and is used as an indicator of continuing reliance on the family for elderly care, the marital status of co-residing children suggests that a remarkable proportion of co-residence reflects the continuation of the original nuclear family, rather than a newly formed extended family.

Furthermore, the following analyses examine living arrangements from the viewpoint of surviving children. Table 3.3 highlights the profiles of the children (a total of 3,128 cases).[4] It is notable that the average number of children is significantly lower (1.8 children) than their parents (4.1 children), reflecting both the sharp fertility reduction in Thailand and the fact that some children have not yet completed their reproduction. Also, a notable portion of children, about 27 percent, are still never-married. Table 3.4 shows that the prevalence of non-marriage is quite high, even among older children: 31.6 percent (aged 30 to 39), 18.7 percent (aged 40 to 49), and 14.5 percent (aged 50 and over). This implies that a sizable number of children are not marrying at all, rather than marrying late.

The proportion of elderly people co-residing with children varies greatly according to the marital status of their children. According to Table 3.5, while as much as 75.9 percent of never-married children live with their parents, only 26.6 percent of ever-married children do so. When never-married children are not living with their parents, they tend

---

4   The children's data were provided by elderly respondents during the interviews.

Table 3.3 Weighted means and percentages of the characteristics of surviving adult children (S.E. in parentheses)

Variables Percentages (S.E.)	# (S.E.)	Unweighted n	
Mean age (in years)	41.1 (0.334)		
Sex			
Male		1,552	50.1 (0.011)
Female		1,572	49.8 (0.011)
Unknown		4	0.1 (0.001)
Marital status			
Never-married		839	26.8 (0.015)
Ever-married		2,266	72.7 (0.014)
Unknown		23	0.5 (0.002)
Number of children (among ever-married)	1.76 (0.033)		

The total number of cases is 3,128.
Total number of cases for age is 3,036 because 92 cases have missing values for this variable.

Table 3.4 Weighted percentages by marital status and age category (unweighted n in parentheses)

	Age categories				
Marital status	15–19	20–29	30–39	4049	50+
Never-married	100.0 (18)	69.6 (180)	31.6 (336)	18.7 (214)	14.5 (80)
Ever-married	0.0 (0)	30.4 (88)	68.4 (701)	81.3 (972)	85.5 (439)
Total	100 (18)	100 (268)	100 (1,037)	100 (1,186)	100 (519)

The total number of cases is 3,028.
A total of 100 cases (3.2 percent of the total child sample) are excluded due to missing values for age and/or marital status.

Table 3.5 Weighted percentages for place of residence, by marital status of the children (unweighted *n* in parentheses)

	Marital Status		
	Never-married	Ever-married	Total
Place of residence			
Same house with parents	75.9 (646)	26.6 (613)	39.7 (1,259)
Same compound with parents	0.6 (4)	2.8 (72)	2.2 (76)
Same *soi*	0.7 (4)	5.7 (127)	4.3 (131)
Same district	2.9 (22)	8.5 (195)	7.0 (217)
In Bangkok	9.8 (87)	35.0 (771)	28.1 (858)
Outside of Bangkok	7.2 (53)	17.6 (404)	14.8 (457)
Abroad	1.9 (16)	2.6 (57)	2.4 (73)

The total number of cases is 3,105 cases.
The 23 cases of children whose marital status (2 cases) or place of residence (21 cases) is unknown are not included.

to live fairly far away from the parental home, either in a different district within Bangkok or in another province. The results cover families at different stages of the family cycle, so it is natural that not all co-residence involves a married child. However, with a growing proportion of never-married children typically not leaving their homes, co-residence with a single child seems to have become more common in Bangkok.

Results of multivariate analyses: Predicting co-residence

This section shows the results of logistic regression analyses to evaluate the effect of the reduction in the number of children elderly people have on co-residence. The model here also emphasizes the children's characteristics in order to examine co-residence from the perspective of both the elderly and their children. Table 3.6 presents the weighted means and percentages of the independent variables included.

Living arrangements: Household type is divided into the dichotomous groupings of co-residence with an adult child and non-co-residence, taking the value of one for co-residence and zero otherwise.

The number of surviving adult children: The number of surviving adult children was recorded. Stepchildren and adopted children were also counted as children. This is the main variable of interest for this analysis.

Age and sex: The birth year of the respondent was recorded using the Buddhist year (Christian calendar year, plus 543 years), and the interviewer coded the current age. In this analysis, people who were aged 60 years or older on their last birthday were included as elderly persons; these are people who were born in and before 1944 in the Western calendar.[5] Sex is coded as 1) Male, or 2) Female.

---

5 Although most of the respondents did not have a problem providing their birth year, when the respondent was uncertain, the Chinese animal calendar was used to identify the year of birth.

Marital status: Marital status is coded as 1) Never-married; 2) Married (regardless of any official marriage registration); 3) Widowed; and 4) Divorced (regardless of the official paperwork status).

Source of income: The main sources of income are coded as 1) Work; 2) Unearned sources (pensions, savings, and rent); 3) Spouse (including income from relatives, excluding children); and 4) Children. This variable is included to examine the impacts of economic independence on co-residence.

Homeownership: The ownership status of the currently lived-in house is recorded as 1) Owned or 2) Rented, and the person owning the house or paying rent is identified as 1) Respondent him/herself or spouse; 2) Relatives, excluding children; 3) Other non-related people; and 4) Children. Homeownership status takes the value of 1) Yes, when respondents or their spouses own a house in their name, as opposed to children's or other people's names; or 2) No, when a respondent does not own a house under his or her own (or a spouse's) name or rents a house.

Health status: The current health status of a respondent was measured using the Activities of Daily Living (ADL) index. Based on the Katz ADL measure, the ADLs used in this analysis include a total of six daily tasks: taking a bath (shower), putting on clothes, going to the toilet, walking around the house, getting up from a bed (or the place where the respondent sleeps), and eating food. Respondents were asked about their ability to perform each task, and their responses were recorded as 1)

Unable to perform, 2) Able to perform with help from other people, or 3) Able to perform without help. Health status is then coded as 1) Has functional problem(s), if the respondent cannot perform one or more of the ADL tasks or requires help to perform the tasks; or 2) Does not have a functional problem, if the respondent can perform all of the tasks without help.

The following information for children was collected through the elderly parents, and attributes for 3,128 children were incorporated in the analyses.

Sex and marital status of children: The sex and marital status of each child were identified and the information included in the model was whether elderly parents have a child who is a married male, married female, never-married male, or never-married female.[6]

Educational level of children: The educational level of children is divided into these categories: 1) No or elementary education; 2) Secondary education; 3) Post-secondary education (more than high school, but less than a B.A.); and 4) B.A. or higher.

Employment status of children: The employment status of each child is reported as 1) Employed or 2) Unemployed.

---

6   Widowed, divorced, or separated children are not considered in this analysis because preliminary analyses suggest that the proportion of these children represented in the data (1.6 percent) is low.

Table 3.6 Weighted means and percentages of predictive variables used in the logistic regression of co-residence with an adult child, among elderly people with an adult child

Variables		Means (S.E.)	Percentages (S.E.)
Elderly characteristics			
Number of adult children alive		3.96 (0.088)	
Age in years		70.5 (0.239)	
Sex (categorical)			
	Male		38.9 (0.015)
	Female		61.1 (0.015)
Marital status (categorical)			
	Married		60.8 (0.026)
	Widowed		32.5 (0.022)
	Divorced		6.7 (0.011)
Source of income (categorical)			
	Work		28.1 (0.020)
	Pension/saving/rent		22.9 (0.013)
	Spouse		9.4 (0.005)
	Children		39.6 (0.034)
Homeownership (categorical)			
	Yes		58.9 (0.028)
	No		41.1 (0.028)
Health status (categorical)			
	Have ADL problems		6.2 (0.011)
	No ADL problems		93.8 (0.011)

Children's characteristics

Sex and marital status (percentage of elderly with)

Married male child	73.2 (0.016)
Married female child	69.6 (0.018)
Never-married male child	35.8 (0.023)
Never-married female child	39.0 (0.021)

Educational level (percentage of elderly with a child who has)

No or elementary education	30.1 (0.003)
Secondary education	39.0 (0.023)
Post-secondary education	39.3 (0.022)
B.A. or higher	60.3 (0.031)

Employment status (percentage of elderly with)

Unemployed child	24.6 (0.017)

The total number of cases is 1,038.

Table 3.7 Logistic regression of co-residence with an adult child, among elderly people with an adult child

		Model 1		Model 2	
Predictive variables		coeff	SE	coeff	SE
Number of adult children [a]		0.129	0.053**	—	—
Age [a]		-0.029	0.016*	-0.013	0.015
Sex	Male	-0.352	0.208*	-0.478	0.221**
	Female [b]	—	—	—	—
Marital status	Widowed	-0.330	0.335	-0.402	0.336
	Divorced	-1.260	0.346***	-1.422	0.349****
	Married [b]	—	—	—	—
Source of income	Work	-1.262	0.321****	-1.513	0.344****
	Pension/saving/rent	-0.772	0.301***	-0.895	0.337***
	Spouse	-2.073	0.353****	-2.368	0.370****
	Children [b]	—	—	—	—
Homeownership	Yes	0.355	0.233	0.412	0.259
	No [b]	—	—	—	-
ADL status	Have ADL problems	0.595	0.514	0.775	0.520
	No ADL problems [b]	—	—	—	—
Have married male					
	Yes	—	—	-0.272	0.310
	No [b]	—	—	—	
Have married female					
	Yes	—	—	-0.418	0.320
	No [b]	—	—	—	—

Have never-married male				
Yes	—	—	1.087	0.299***
No [b]	—	—	—	—
Have never-married female				
Yes	—	—	0.963	0.287***
No [b]	—	—	—	—
Have child with no education or elementary education				
Yes	—	—	0.539	0.237**
No [b]	—	—	—	—
Have child with secondary education				
Yes	—	—	-0.014	0.258
No [b]	—	—	—	—
Have child with post-secondary education				
Yes	—	—	0.151	0.286
No [b]	—	—	—	—
Have child with a B.A. or higher				
Yes	—	—	0.101	0.215
No [b]	—	—	—	—
Have unemployed child				
Yes	—	—	0.328	0.369
No [b]	—	—	—	—
Intercept	4.249	1.173***	3.438	1.151***
Pseudo R^2	0.132		0.238	
Sample size	1,038		1,038	

Four cases of never-married elderly people who adopted a child are excluded, so no never-married elderly are included in the analysis.
[a] denotes continuous variable, and [b] designates reference category.
*$p<0.10$, **$p<0.05$, ***$p<0.01$, **** $p<0.001$.

Since co-residence with an adult child is a dichotomous outcome variable, logistic regression techniques are used to estimate the independent effects of predictive variables. Two models are tested, one including characteristics of the elderly only, and the other including characteristics of both the elderly and children.

The main purpose of the first model (that includes only the characteristics of the elderly) is to test the impacts of the availability of children, expressed as the number of adult children an elderly person has. As expected, the number of adult children has a significantly positive effect on co-residence, controlling for other predictor variables. It is estimated that the chance of co-residence increases by 1.14 times with a one-person increase in the number of adult children. Among other demographic characteristics of the elderly, the effects of being divorced have a highly negative significance: the probability of co-residence for a divorced elderly person is 0.28 times that of married elderly people. Neither the age of the elderly nor their health status shows the expected effect. The result suggests that the health status of the elderly is not a significant indicator for co-residence; elderly people who have an ADL problem are no more likely to live with a child than elderly people who do not have a problem.[7] Moreover, the age of the elderly person has the

---

7 However, the impacts of poor health may not be properly reflected, considering the low proportion of elderly people with an ADL problem (6.2

opposite direction from the hypothesized positive effect with moderate statistical significance (at $p<0.10$).

The elderly person's sources of income are shown to be an important determinant of co-residence. Compared with an elderly person whose main source of income is from children, an elderly person who has an independent source of income (work, unearned income, and spouse) has a significantly smaller likelihood of living with a child. The social meaning of income from work and from unearned sources is quite different in the Thai context. Having work as a main source of income usually indicates that the elderly individual still has to use his/her body to earn a living, and subsequently implies lower economic status.[8] On the other hand, when pension, savings, or rent is the main source of income, this suggests that the person had some kind of prestigious employment that provides social security (i.e., being a civil servant) or wealth that can produce a monthly income; in either case, income from unearned sources implies a higher social class than that of the majority of the population.

Given this information, the negative significance of each source of independent income can be interpreted differently. For those elderly

---

percent).
8 Among the elderly people whose main source of income is from work (301 cases), more than 80 percent are engaged in a job requiring physical labor, such as hawking, cleaning, construction, and craft work.

with income from unearned sources, the negative effect of income may be a reflection of their desire to live independently and of their ability to do so. The model estimates that elderly people who have unearned independent income (pension, savings, or rent) have about a 50 percent lower likelihood of co-residence than elderly people with income from children. On the other hand, the negative significance for elderly people whose source of income is work may mean that answering the needs of the elderly and reducing their costs of living is not an important factor for co-residence; if these needs were determinative, economically struggling elderly people should be more likely to be living with a child.

The highly significant negative effect of having income from work leads to the question of whether the needs of the elderly have to be considered in relation to the condition of their children. The concept of "lucrilocality" or the tendency of newly married children to live with more financially capable parents (Chamratrithirong et al. 1988) may be helpful here. If married children assess the economic conditions of all parties involved (both parents and themselves), and decide to live where there are greater resources, then elderly parents who are poor may have fewer chances to live with a child because they do not have sufficient resources to attract one to live with them.

Next, the second model which included both children's and elderly people's characteristics was considered. For this model, in addition to the predictive variables included in the first model, gender, marital status, educational level, and employment status of children are introduced as the socio-demographic characteristics of children, while the number of adult children is dropped as it is associated with having a child of the respective characteristics. With the introduction of children's characteristics, the age of the elderly loses its original moderate significance. However, the sex of the elderly becomes statistically significant at the $p<0.05$ level, showing that elderly males are less likely to live with a child than elderly females. This finding, which emerged only after including children's characteristics, should be noted because the literature on children's obligations to repay debts to parents often focuses on debt to mothers who have given birth to children (e.g. Van Esterik 1996).

Another important result of this model is the strong positive impact of the presence of a never-married child on co-residence. The likelihood of co-residence of elderly people with a never-married male child is three times higher than that of elderly people who do not have any never-married male children. Similarly, the odds for the elderly with a never-married female child are 2.6 times those for the elderly with no never-married female children. It is apparent from the analysis that children's marital status is a major determinant of co-residence for the elderly. This model, which includes children's characteristics, suggests that despite a significantly reduced number of children per elderly parent in future generations, as long as one child remains single, that child can contribute to the continuity of co-residence.

Another significant finding from the analysis is that elderly people with a less-educated child are much more likely to live with a child. Elderly people who have a child with either no education or with only elementary school education are about 1.7 times more likely to be in co-residence. Moreover, the finding that having a better-educated child (secondary education, post-secondary education, or a B.A. or higher) does not affect the chance of co-residence indicates that better education does not affect children's decisions about living independently from parents. This may be because better-educated Thais, particularly women, have a higher probability of remaining single (Guest and Tan 1994), so having educated children would not negatively affect co-residence.

Ethnographic Insights: Qualitative Results

This section will focus on the recurrent themes that emerged from the in-depth interviews regarding the underlying structures that support co-residence in Thai society.[9] The following analyses investigate issues that have not been adequately captured in the above multivariate analyses and help us to understand the determinants of co-residence in a more

---

9   NUD*IST (Non-numerical Unstructured Data Indexing Searching and Theorizing) was used for the following qualitative data analysis to organize, explore, and categorize data.

holistic way. Data for the analyses were derived from English-translated transcriptions of the in-depth interviews collected from a total of 28 Thai people. Those interviewed included five pairs of elderly parents and one each of their ever-married children (including one divorced child), and six pairs of elderly parents and one each of their never-married children. Additionally, six elderly people who were not living with an adult child were interviewed, including individuals who lived completely alone, lived with a friend, lived with nephews and nieces, lived with a spouse and grandchildren, or lived only with grandchildren. In selecting interview candidates from the entire sample of elderly people, special care was taken to choose interviewees from a wide variety of socio-economic backgrounds.[10]

The wrong question

One of the main objectives of the interview was to discover the process that led to the elderly person's current living arrangements and

---

10 Different parent-child combinations based on sex and marital status were first listed. Then the parent-child pairs were divided into three categories of economic-status (low, middle, and high), based on such indicators as educational level, types of housing, and employment histories. Finally, the eligible respondents for each socio-economic category were selected, taking into account issues that are important for recruiting interviewees for in-depth interviews, including the ability of respondents to express themselves and their willingness to allocate time for the interview.

to understand the attitudes, opinions, and actions that led to these arrangements. The author approached elderly people as individual decision-makers, influenced by the literature that focuses on individual decision-making as a basic mechanism for living arrangement outcomes (e.g. Mutchler and Burr 1991). Thus, one line of questioning focused on the elderly as actors, including questions such as "Why did you decide to live with this child?" and "Why did you choose to live with a child, not with your husband only, for example?"

Interview sessions and later analyses of the interview data, however, made the author realize that she might have been asking questions from the wrong perspective. Instead of asking questions from the viewpoint of "your choices and decisions," a more appropriate approach might have been to try to understand the circumstances that led each elderly person to live in the current arrangement. For example, in the case below, an elderly woman explains that she lost a co-residing single daughter and now lives with a married son. Only hearing the story from the co-residing child makes it clear why this child came to be the new co-residing partner. Because the process of co-residence is often a result of incidents beyond the elderly person's control, it is difficult for them to describe it as their decision.

> AN ELDERLY MOTHER: Since 1964, when I came out to Bangkok, I have been selling things by carrying baskets of goods.

I took my kids with me to Bangkok because my husband took a new wife in the countryside. So, I left him and came here to this house. She (her child with whom she had co-resided) also came here and lived with me since she was 12 years old. But when she was 25 years old, she got hit by a car and died. (Yanawa 6-a)

HER CO-RESIDING MARRIED SON: I have six siblings, but one is dead. That one was living with my mother. I moved out once, but my sister (who was living with the mother) died. Then, no one was there to take care of the mother when she was sick or like that. By then, I was already married and had moved out. We need a room for each family, right? So, we male children had to move out, letting my sister live here. (In answering whether other siblings wanted to come back to the house when the sister died). It is, how do you say, circumstances. The oldest one was living in the countryside. He has a family there. He had already left Bangkok and he did not have a job here that he could pick up. This was one reason (for the brother not to come back). On the other hand, I could work at the same place as before after the move. (Yanawa 6-b)

Another important factor is the often-emphasized preference of Thai elderly people to live with a child. The preference for co-residence among the Thai elderly is well known and has been extensively reported on in past studies. The author was originally skeptical about the pervasiveness and the degree of this preference, but the elderly people she came to know during the fieldwork, either through direct interviews or informal conversations before or afterward, all expressed a desire to live with their children. Thai elderly, from poor to wealthy, want to live with children if the situation allows.

Taking "preference" as a starting point provides a more productive way of approaching the determinants of living arrangements. Instead of examining co-residence as a choice of the elderly, the author tried to discover the preferences, choices, and conditions of children, assuming that the elderly were ready to live with a child as long as the child was also ready and able. Therefore, the following analyses are organized around the premise that co-residence in Thailand is supported by elderly people's preference for co-residence and the conditions of their children, as these would determine whether co-residence is a realistic option. It is not, however, intended to imply that the elderly people are totally helpless in determining their living arrangements; they also take direct and indirect actions, as will be evident in the following analyses.

Is there a "good child"?

A theme that emerges from the interviews is the importance of having a child who recognizes the concept of *bun khun*, or children's obligations to repay parents. The concept of *bun khun* has been discussed in the literature as the most important factor for defining parent-child relationships (Rabibhadana 1984), and having a good child who knows *bun khun* has been seen as the key to co-residence in Thailand (Knodel et al. 1994; Knodel et al. 1995). Data from the interviews provided further insights into this concept and revealed the weight it has in determining elderly people's living arrangements. After discussing how the concept of *bun khun* works, the living arrangement outcomes of elderly individuals with "good" children who practice *bun khun,* and of those with "bad" children who are said to have ignored *bun khun,* are compared below.

The passage comes from an interview with a never-married elderly woman with some established wealth, who currently lives with a lifelong nanny (who is also an elderly person) and several nieces and nephews. Her story clearly shows why she was the one, out of many siblings, who lived with the mother and took care of her until her death.

> Taking care of my mother was my happiness. We believe that because parents raise us, we should take care of them. I had the chance to return *bun khun* to my parents. I did everything for my parents. I felt happy rather than irritated about my situation.

I could not think of moving out of the house like the others. I also wanted to take care of her. My siblings saw that I was already taking care of her, and she was not in a troubled condition. They knew my mother could live like that with me. So they did not bother to come and take care of her. They did not need to ask for money and things from my mother; that was already good enough.

(In answer to whether she had been asked by the mother or siblings to take responsibility). No. It was from my own feelings that I decided to live with her. One person was needed to take care of her. I had three older siblings and three younger ones. But the three older ones had chosen other ways already, after marriage. As for the younger three, they were still studying. So the one left was the middle one, me, who was not too young, but also not too established as an adult yet. (Watana 8-c)

The next passage comes from another never-married woman in her mid-thirties who lives with her elderly mother and the young son of her divorced and now-ordained younger brother. She is a college graduate and has a relatively good white-collar job at an international company. She has bought a house with her savings and provides for all household expenses, including schooling fees for the nephew. For her, supporting not only her mother but also her nephew is a natural thing to do as an able member of the family, and she is happy to do so.

> I would like to take care of my mother. I think she is very old. So I have to look after her. This is my responsibility, like any daughter has. We Thai people think we have to take responsibility. We have to take responsibility for our parents. I think, my mother, she has been taking care of me since I was a little baby. She must have been more tired than I am tired now, I think so. Thus, I can do everything for her as much as I can. Fortunately, I have a good job to support the family. It is because my mother gave me this opportunity; she sent me to school and to university so that I could get a good job. That is why I have to take good care of her.
>
> My nephew is also my responsibility. He is my duty because I am his aunt; he is with me now. Sometimes I feel tired, but when I see his face, my nephew's, he needs my care. So I think it is OK. Yes, yes I accept this. My nephew is now in my family. So it is not strange that everything is on me, live on me. Also, the reason why I can do everything for them is because I love them, everyone in my family. (Huaykhwang 2-b, interviewed in English)

Elderly parents who managed to have a good child, as in the above examples, and who consequently safely achieved co-residence, seem to know with confidence that their old-age living arrangement is secure. Even though elderly parents usually do not have an effective way to directly manipulate adult children, they are conscious of what they have provided to their children and also know how successful the past investment has been. In a sense, whether one can live with a child in old age is the final test of how well past efforts in rearing the children have turned out.

> THE MOTHER OF A NEVER-MARRIED DAUGHTER:
> Some children marry and forget about parents. But my daughter does not do that to me because she used to tell me, "Mother, you only have two children. If we do not love you, who is going to love you? Who is going to love mother? Who is going to take care of mother?" (Huaykhwang 2-a)

> THE MOTHER OF A NEVER-MARRIED SON, A MARRIED SON, THREE NEVER-MARRIED DAUGHTERS, AND A MARRIED DAUGHTER:
> After the children became 20 and finished studying, things got easier for me. They work and give me money. Whatever the amount they make, they give me money. (In answer to whether she had told them to do so). No, I do not need to tell them. They give the money by themselves. All I taught them was to study hard

and work hard. But they know seeing the mother going through troubles (that they have to repay *bun khun*). They give money voluntarily out of what they make; keep some for themselves to use, and give me the rest. Some children do not give in Thailand. Some children are good, right? Good children give, depending on their minds. (Bangna 9-a)

Of course, in reality, not all children become "good" children who know *bun khun*. In contrast to elderly parents with *bun khun*-minded children, the elderly with "bad" children who do not recognize *bun khun* expressed their frustrations and anger against their children. In the case below, of the five children who live with this elderly mother, three are dependent on the mother. When the author talked with her, she expressed her frustration with the situation and aggressively criticized her children for not knowing *bun khun*. In her case, and many other similar cases from low-income families, having many children does not seem to ensure a secure old age. Rather, the number of children seems to have increased her problems.

My children do not return *bun khun*. Only the fourth one and two females know it. The others, they do not know. I have been taking care of myself all the time. I raised them. After they grew up, I thought it would be *sabaay* (comfortable), but they are eating off of me. Here, the house is mine and they do not need to pay even for bills. They do not accept leaving the house, either.

The oldest one moved out. The second child, a female, she is now separated. She lives with us. She has one child, and he is also with me. The daughter pays for his school, but food is on me. It is oh-so difficult; buying food is *lamba* (difficult). The third one, male and married, he lives here, but he does not deal with me. He eats by himself. He has a *feen* (girlfriend or wife), but seeing us having difficulties, they do not involve themselves with us. And the fourth one is a male, not married. I can get some money from him. At the end of the month, he gives me 1,000 baht.[11] When I do not have money, I can ask him for an additional 200 to 300 baht. He is renting a house inside a *soi* (lane). He drives a car. The fifth one has been living with her father (respondent's ex-husband); I have not seen her for a long time. The sixth and seventh, single girls, are fine. And the last one is a female, married. She has two children that she abandoned with me. They have not thought that there is no one to support their mother. (Khlongtoey 10-a)

---

11   About 3,000 yen at the exchange rate of that time.

Non-marriage and the concept of bun khun

One of the most important findings from the children's interviews is that the concept and practice of *bun khun* seem to encourage children, especially female children who do not have a chance to send *bun* to parents by ordination, to continue to live with parents as unmarried adults. The never-married children frequently mentioned their attachment to their families and a desire to care for their elderly parents as a reason for their single status. Although these never-married children come from a variety of backgrounds, their logic is quite consistent. They see marriage as a potential obstacle to properly caring for elderly parents. In their view, marriage is something that brings more dependents to support, and more worries and troubles to deal with. These children are not necessarily opposed to marriage per se, but they give greater priority to the family of origin rather than to a new family of procreation.

> A NEVER-MARRIED MALE CHILD IN HIS FORTIES LIVING WITH PARENTS: People say that single people want to get into marriage, but married people want to get out of it. It is better to live with freedom. If I marry, I have to worry about my wife. But my mother is getting old day by day. In any case, as long as my mother is alive and healthy, I am proud. I am not rich but I am proud. (Dingdaeng 10-b)

A NEVER-MARRIED FEMALE CHILD IN HER MID-THIRTIES LIVING WITH HER MOTHER, HER DEPENDENT SIBLINGS, AND THEIR CHILDREN: (in answer to why she remains single) I have other obligations (than marrying) to support the family. I do not want to have my own family. I want to live like this. Moving out and living an outside life, I have not yet thought about it. (Khlongtoey 11-b)

A NEVER-MARRIED ELDERLY WOMAN LIVING WITH A NANNY AND YOUNGER RELATIVES: Our family's financial status allowed me to live without marrying or working. And (when I was younger) I realized that marriage would take time away from being with my parents. If I were to marry, my husband and his family may not be nice to us. I do not need a marriage. I think that marriage is not at all necessary. Marriage has not been a priority in my life; taking care of my parents had the highest priority. (Watana 8-c)

Apparent in these quotes is that these *bun khun*-oriented never-married children have strong attachments to their family of origin, particularly to the mother, but also to other dependent younger relatives. In fact, the system of *bun khun* is built upon children's attachment to and sense of responsibility for the family of origin. Parents cannot fully receive the benefits of *bun khun* if the allegiance of their children has moved to the new family. The marriage of a child, and the resulting presence of the child-in-law and associated new family, often introduce a source of conflict in the family of origin. With the marriage of a child, parents have to face the potential danger that the child may no longer be able to practice *bun khun* to its full extent. Worse, the child may forget about *bun khun* entirely. During the interviews, some children, particularly those with low incomes, openly pointed out this problem.

> A MARRIED FEMALE CHILD LIVING WITH HER PARENTS, HUSBAND, AND THREE CHILDREN: I think loving my family is one thing, and loving my parents is another. However, sometimes we have problems. If I give too much money to my parents, it is a problem for my family. But if I cut my parents off, that is too sorry for them. If I take my family, I feel sorry for my parents. I have to take my parents, too. (Wangtonglarn 9-b)

> A DIVORCED FEMALE CHILD LIVING WITH HER FATHER AND SEVERAL CHILDREN: I already told my siblings that even if I have a lot of money, I would not let them come back (to live with the father) because they put more importance on their spouses. Like my brother, he likes his wife and children more, so they moved out and he does not live with

my father. His wife does not get along with my father, so they cannot live together. Because I do not have a family, I can live with my father. Living alone or living with kids only, you can live (with your father). If you have a family, you move out and cannot live with your father. (Ratburana 5-b)

Accumulation of bun in context: Merit-making, ordination, and the mother

For men, becoming ordained at least once in their lifetime is regarded as being highly important in Thai society. It is particularly important because of the Buddhist belief that the merits gained in the process of being a monk are transferred to the mother of the ordained man. It is said that the accumulation of merit (*bun*) is achieved through meritorious action defined in the Buddhist normative system (Kirsch 1982). In the field, the author encountered many different occasions when local people, old and young, talked about the incidence of ordination and issues around merit-making. For example, one day the *phii liang* (nanny) the author had for her son mentioned that her husband, a taxi driver, had gotten ordained over the weekend. She seemed to be very proud of the event. The author was first surprised to find her referring to him using special Thai words that were only used for respected people. The nanny explained that because now that her husband was a monk even for a temporary period (he was to be ordained during the rainy season), she was not allowed to treat him in a regular way. Then she asked if the author could give her a pay rise. She asked for extra money because monks are prohibited from earning money, and she was now the only income earner in the household. She looked quite uneasy about her financial situation, but she was still extremely happy that her husband was finally able to be ordained and make merit. From this incident, the author came to understand the mixed feelings Thai women have about the ordination of men in the household. Ordination is definitely a wonderful event in terms of gaining respect and merit, but is also a flight from worldly things, and women are left behind with the worries of daily life. Since the author was so curious about the ordination, my research assistant further explained to me that a man decides to become ordained when he feels he is ready, and it is not appropriate to stop him once he decides. Also, he added that once a man is ordained, no one knows when he will be ready to come back to the worldly life; it depends on the "ripeness" of the man.

The author had another interesting incident about merit-making with this research assistant. He and the author spent almost two months together interviewing elderly people all over Bangkok. One day, we interviewed an elderly man who was financially struggling. After the interview, we stopped by a noodle shop on the street to have lunch. The assistant then asked me, "Yoshie, do you want to bring a bowl of noodles to the elderly man?" The author was a little reluctant, as it seemed that there would be no end once she started to buy lunch for every poor elderly person met. However, the author followed the suggestion. After he delivered the noodles to the elderly man, my assistant said to me, "You are lucky today. Because of that elderly man, you could get a chance to make merit. I am happy to see Yoshie making merit, and I could also make merit by advising you to buy lunch for him." The author was very surprised to hear his comments. In the course of fieldwork, however, she slowly started to understand that merit-making does not just mean formal meritorious acts like giving alms to monks in the morning, but that all "good" behaviors are counted as merit-making. In this merit-making system, a man's ordination is the largest act of merit-making.

Ordination is particularly special, as merit gained by ordination is believed to be transferred to the mother of the man. The author clearly remembers an episode involving the transfer of merit and the big smile of an elderly woman. In the field, stories of grandparents taking care of grandchildren appeared repeatedly, particularly in poor neighborhoods. The author visited one of these grandmothers who was financially and physically supporting a five-year-old grandson, the child of her son. As expected, she was struggling to make ends meet every day, and she told the history of her son being irresponsible and doing what he was not supposed to do. However, when the author asked where he was, the grandmother was delighted to tell me that he was at a temple as a monk. She proudly explained that he decided to be a monk and live at a temple not too far from her home. Her joy was to visit the monk at the temple with a donation gift box that contained soaps, candles, and other daily necessities. The elderly woman seemed to have forgiven her son for his past bad conduct. This woman's story is a good example that demonstrates the relationships between Buddhism, men, and elderly mothers. In the framework of the merit-making system, an irresponsible and badly behaved man is given a chance to redeem himself to pay off his bad deeds by becoming a monk, making him a "good" boy who sends merit to his mother.

Conclusions

The demographic conditions of Bangkok, Thailand, have provided an ideal setting to examine the impacts of demographic changes on the living arrangements of the elderly. The results of the analyses confirm that the number of surviving children is a significant determinant of co-residence; elderly people who have more children have a better chance of living with at least one child. Furthermore, the analyses of the characteristics of their children show that having a never-married child, either male or female, is a powerful determinant of co-residence. The finding indicates that despite the lowered number of children in the future, as long as one child remains never married, that child can live with the parent. The positive impact of never-married children is particularly significant, given the noticeable increase in the number of never-married people in Bangkok. That is, the increasing prevalence of never-married children may contribute to the maintenance of co-residence, mitigating the expected negative impacts of fewer children.

In addition to the marital status of children, their willingness to recognize their obligations to repay parents in the form of old-age support is hugely important in considering co-residence outcomes. How much a child wants to repay his or her parents is related to the concept of the accumulation of merit (*bun*). Accumulation of merit is one of the most important activities that Thai people want to do in the Buddhist norm system. Merit-making is not only achieved by formal actions such as giving alms to monks in the morning or visiting temples; every act that is meritorious is counted for merit-making. Out of various merit-making acts, the ordination of a man is regarded as a huge merit-making act because merit earned this way is transferred to the mother of the man. Because the fundamental preference of elderly parents is to live with a child if it is a viable option, the critical factor is whether children recognize the concept of *bun khun*. If no child recognizes *bun khun*, then having many children does not necessarily help ensure co-residence in old age.

Findings suggest that the impacts of never-married children on old-age co-residence need to be carefully evaluated from both short-term and long-term perspectives. In terms of ensuring "co-residence" in Thailand, rising rates of non-marriage and high involvement of these never-married children in co-residence are positive factors. However, the most problematic consequence of low fertility and emerging high non-marriage rates may be the loss of the rich circle of relatives that functions as a powerful secondary source of elderly support when children are not available. The option of living with a relative may not be easy or even possible in the future. Given the already low fertility rates in Thailand, the sharply rising rates of non-marriages should sound an alarm and not be ignored, despite the possible short-term benefits of having never-married children available for elderly support.

Chapter 4

SEXUAL AND REPRODUCTIVE BEHAVIOR AMONG SINGLE MALES IN JAPAN

Chapter 4 SEXUAL AND REPRODUCTIVE BEHAVIOR AMONG SINGLE MALES IN JAPAN

In past studies, the issue of sexlessness has been discussed in the context of being "sexless" with a specific partner, particularly the spouse. However, it does not necessarily mean that the "sexless" person has been free from sexual activity. So it is important to examine the partner(s) of sexual activities from a wider perspective to obtain a fuller picture of sexuality and reproduction in Japanese society. This chapter focuses on the sexual behaviors of heterosexual single Japanese males. The voices of a total of 31 men highlight the reality and problems of sexual and reproductive behaviors in contemporary Japan. The following analyses are based on eight sessions of focus group discussions conducted in 2022 (see Chapter 2 for methodological details). The participants were healthy men aged 20 to 39 years old, who were not students, and who lived in different parts of Japan. Participants included both university and high school graduates. As for marital status, all participants were single, apart from two men who were married.[1]

---

1   Sessions were recorded with the permission of participants using the Zoom recording function. The quotes in this chapter were translated by the author from the transcribed discussions in Japanese to English. Although two married men were included in the sessions, their data have been excluded from the analyses here.

Meaning of Sexual Activities: Social Sexuality and Solo Sexuality

Sex with a specific and with non-specific partners

The phenomenon of sexlessness discussed in Chapter 1 is often viewed as an example of the decline in sexual activities and desires in Japan. However, as the following data from focus group discussions suggest, the reality may not be the case when we expand the scope of sexlessness, especially when we try to capture variations of sexual partners. Sociological discourses show the role and significance of romantic love ideology which is often said to have become the backbone of modern families. Akagawa (1995) argues that among different sexual behaviors, such as masturbation, homosexuality, prostitution, marital sexual intercourse, premarital sex, and sex outside of marriage, what is acceptable and what is regulated, have historically changed. That is, a "standard" sexual behavior is a social product. Out of the various sexual behaviors, in modern Japanese society, sexual activities between married couples have been reinforced as acceptable, and they have been promoted as the norm in conjunction with the so-called romantic love ideology. Akagawa elaborates that a family built by the wife and husband is socially constructed as a place full of sexual desire and sex, a situation he calls "eroticization of sexual behavior in marriage" (Akagawa 1995:160).

This situation, however, once seemingly weaved into Japanese society, started to fall apart. Ueno Chizuko (1987) noted the downfall of the "Trinity of Love-Sex-Marriage" in Japanese society. According to her, the Japanese never really accepted the romantic love ideology and the associated concept of a modern monogamous middle-class family; there are ample examples observed in Japanese society in which not only men but also women deviate from the sexual norms stipulated by the romantic love ideology. Ueno points out that the love-sex-marriage trinity is an inherently unnatural connection, a product of modern sexuality norms that make heterosexual, monogamous (=exclusive) relationships natural (Ueno 1987). Akagawa (1999) further examines the changes in social discourses regarding merit/demerits and acceptance/refusal of musturbation over the years and suggests the significant role of musturbation as an independent and active sexual behavior in Japan.

The phenomenon of sexlessness observed in recent years can be interpreted as one indication of the disintegration of the above trinity. For example, a study about casual sex and sexlessness among Japanese males (aged 20 to 54) found that inactive sexual activity within committed relationships (wife for married or girlfriend/fiancé for single) is linked to sexual activity outside such relationships. To begin with, the percentage of sexlessness among married men (those who did not have sex in the last month) in this study is as high as the levels found in previous studies, 49 percent. Out of the remaining 51 percent of non-sexless respondents, 36 percent had sex only with the spouse, while 10 percent had sex with a casual partner only (6 percent) or with both casual and non-casual partners (4 percent) (Konishi et al. 2022a).[2]

Konishi et al.'s results on the sexual partner(s) of single men further provide evidence regarding the disintegration of the trinity. Their findings show that out of non-sexless single men,[3] 12 percent of never-married and 22 percent of other single had sex with casual partner(s). In fact, out of all single men, less than 20 percent (17 percent for never-married and 18 percent for others) had sex only with a non-casual partner (that is, girlfriend/boyfriend or fiancé). As for variations of the partner(s), although 73 percent of never-married men had sex with a specific partner (girlfriend/boyfriend or fiancé), 9 percent had sex with someone "more than a friend but less than a girlfriend/boyfriend," 15 percent had sex with a "friend(s) with benefits," 8 percent with a friend or casual acquaintance, 5 percent with someone for a one-night stand, and 11 percent with a commercial sex worker(s)(Konishi et al. 2022a). These data suggest that, first, a majority of single men are sexless, and second, for those who do have sex, having sex and committed relationships are not necessarily linked, and their sexual partner(s) are often outside of committed relationships and/or are a non-specific partner(s).

The following qualitative data from the focus group discussions reveal the meaning of these variations. In the quantitative data above,

---

2 6 percent is missing information about the number of partners.
3 As much as 64 percent (never-married) and 51 percent (others) were sexless.

for statistical analyses, sexual activity with different types of partners is dichotomously categorized into "non-casual" and "casual." There is, however, a different social significance associated with various types of partners outside of committed relationships, beyond just being casual. The quotes below illustrate exploratory steps men may take when they meet a woman.

> Basically, the initial contact with any person is the same. From there, I try to figure out things like whether we have something in common, similarities in the standards of living, etc. to see if things match as you interact with the woman. If you have a different life orientation, the relationship will become just that (= having sex), and you will not move forward from there. If I feel at home, or at ease with that woman, then I move forward. So, I don't have a clear standard, but I think that's how I separate women. (061913B)

For this man, if the overall match is not great, the relationship with that woman remains casual and that woman can be considered to be a "friend with benefits." Another man's comment further explains a subtle feeling toward a relationship that can be also called "casual." He knows the relationship was ambiguous and he did not have an intention to make it formal (to be a boyfriend and girlfriend) or to clearly end the relationship.

> It is not like I asked her to become my girlfriend or anything like that. We had sex. We went out together for fun too. I do not think it was just a casual relationship for the sake of sex, but we were not in a formal relationship either. It was an ambiguous relationship. (061913A)

When these men were asked the differences between a girlfriend and other women with whom they have sex and/or also go out to have fun, several of them provided similar answers using the ideas of "sharing" and "future."

> Whether having sex comes first or having an agreement to be a girlfriend comes first may vary from person to person. But someone with whom you want to spend time together, including the act of going out and sharing various aspects of one's life, is generally your dating partner (girlfriend). (061913C)

> Someone with whom I am just going out for fun or a woman who is a friend with benefits is a kind of temporary measure with no thought of the future. However, someone I would like to date as my girlfriend is someone whom I can feel that I want to support in the future in various ways. (061910D)

During sessions, talks over so-called "one-night stands" also appeared. When such incidents were mentioned, men typically emphasized mutual agreements of having one-time relations to avoid possible problems. Although SNS and matching apps are highlighted as convenient tools to meet a woman for this purpose, at the same time, they also seem to realize the danger of meeting someone without social context. Regarding precautions, a man explained as below.

> Because that (having problems with a one-night woman) would not be good. So, if I meet someone in person, I may not do it until the end (= have sex) to avoid the risks involved.
> (In response to a question that meeting a woman in real is riskier) Yes, I think that's true. I think both sides (men and women) know that that's dangerous if you don't know how the person is. (071015A)

While meeting a woman and having sex with that person out of your daily social context without knowing reliable personal information can be risky, possible complications of having casual and irresponsible relations within one's community were also pointed out.

> With matching apps, it's possible to do something weird and not see each other again. But with people from work or friends, it's

hard to do that because of the relationship you have afterward. (071710F)

I don't have a friend with benefits, but there were times when I did have one-night sex with a woman. In that case, I don't really want to do it again with that person. In such cases, no strings attached, and I just let it all go after one time. When I was in college, I had a chance to meet and have sex with someone from the same university or someone from my hometown. But if I were to continue with them (without a formal agreement), it would be a little troublesome. I might have to deal with a lot of problems. So, I don't think it would be suitable for me to have sex multiple times with a woman as a "friend with benefits." (071710C)

These voices of single men suggest that having sex with a woman can be just an entrance to different relationships that may or may not develop after having sex. In this sense, it appears that love (feelings) is not a required condition for having sex among these men. However, it should be noted that some men in the focus group sessions were quite clear that they would not have sex before making sure they were in the specific relationship as a boyfriend and girlfriend. Several men were even rather surprised to know that other men could have sex before formally confirming their dating status. In fact, across various sessions, the sense of responsibility and the degree of feelings men want when seeking sexual relations varied significantly depending on the person.

The use of the sex industry is one of the topics that divided opinions and experiences. The first two quotes below were from men who frequent(ed) these services. They indicate that service can be provided by any person available, and it seems that as long as their needs are met, they are content. On the other hand, in the latter two cases, men's desire for some sense of feelings or attachment is expressed. In particular, the last man said he has been visiting this woman for many years regularly, once every one or two months. He claims that he has not had sexual activity with any other women, partially due to his fetish and largely his feelings toward this specific woman. The last quote may be an outlier case, but it does suggest the involvement of feelings even though he and the woman in the sex industry were not in a committed relationship in a traditional sense.

> I went to one of those places which give massages once every two or three months. It was not for a specific person, but rather for anyone whose schedule was open when I wanted to go. (071010B)

> I don't go there all the time, but I go when I don't have a girlfriend. I don't know what else to do. I started going when my seniors at work took me out for a drink and... so I guess that's how I learned to have fun. (071710B)

I am interested, but to be honest, when I look at the cost, I don't think I would be willing to go. Also, in the end, I can't help but think that I don't feel very fulfilled because it's something women do for work. So, I'm not going there. (071715D)

Basically, I have sex with a particular woman. She is a very nice person, and we have even exchanged LINE.[4] Now, it is impossible for me to do it with someone other than her. Anyway, this is the place where I used to go. At that time, I didn't know any women there, so I left it up to the shop. The first person I met there was the person I am meeting now. We had a good match there. Then, I have been going there for a long time. (071010A)

This section highlighted the gradation of feelings and sense of attachment men have toward different types of "casual" relationships. As one man stated, "Having sex does not mean we can automatically step forward to be in the committed relationships" (071713B). So sex can be a starting point, but what is more important and needed for the relationship to move forward is the sense of matching each other, the enjoyment of spending time together, and the vision of a shared future.

---

4   One of the social networking services. It is an application that allows registered users to exchange text messages and make free calls.

Sex as solo act: Preference for masturbation

So far, the sexual behaviors examined have been acts conducted socially, meaning that a man engages in sexual activity with a partner, regardless of the status of their relationship. This section focuses on the other aspect of sexual behavior that is performed by oneself, masturbation. Analyses of one of two online surveys (cross-sectional one and retrospective one), discussed in Chapter 2 on Japanese men's sexual behaviors, suggest that the breakdown of the number of ejaculations in the past month was about 80 percent by masturbation and 20 percent by sexual activity involving a partner (tabulated by the author), showing the predominancy of solo sexual activity. Moreover, based on the retrospective survey, which follows the history of respondents' (both married and single) sexual behavior over 20 years, Akagawa (2024) found that the frequency of sex has declined from 1999 to 2019, while masturbation frequency has not changed or has even increased for each age group (20s, 30s, and 40s). According to him, the average frequency of masturbation for men in their 30s in particular has increased: 123 times in 1999, 135 times in 2009, 139 times in 2014, and 141 times in 2019. Thus, these data on masturbation imply that even though "flight from sex" (Sato 2022) is progressing, it does not mean flight from all sexual activity is happening.

Qualitative information from focus group discussions confirms Japanese men's preference for solo sexual activity. As the following statements suggest, participants of the sessions pointed out the time efficiency of masturbation. Also, in comparison to having sex with a partner, masturbation is perceived as being easier as they can simply focus on the pursuit of their sexual desire, using whatever they like.

> When I do it alone, if I do it quickly, it really only takes five minutes or so. However, when I go to a hotel (with a woman), I stay there for two or three hours after we enter until we leave. (061910C)

> In the case of masturbation, one is completely on one's own, and everything is self-contained. But in the case of sexual activity with a partner, more or less care and effort are required. There are troubles to get to that point, too... (071713B)

> Sex is with a partner, so you have to pay attention to various things. In masturbation, you just have your favorite side dishes (sexual aids), and you can do it while looking at a beautiful woman or something. (061910D)

> (When asked about his favorite types of sexual aids), I think there are various kinds of things. There are videos, but I prefer images, whether two-dimensional or three-dimensional, manga, 18-rated audio, adult games, etc. How often I use each thing is different

though. (071715B)

When talking about the details of sexual aids (*okazu* in Japanese) and one's sexual fantasy, several participants brought up the issue of guilt. On this point, Akagawa (2023a) describes similar feelings referring to a literary work by Yukio Mishima. He explains that the choice of sexual aids for masturbation is a highly private matter, but at the same time, a potential violation of social taboos.

> Video is probably the quickest way. When I'm doing the act (masturbating), I don't think about the woman from my past or the person I currently have feelings for. I think that would be a little disrespectful to them. When I am masturbating, I try to get excited, but thinking of some real people lowers the tension. So basically, I don't do it. (071713B)

In addition, curiously, a participant touched upon an aspect of violence found in one's sexuality. He argued that his sexual fantasy involved cruelty and violence toward women but because he has warm feelings for his partner, having sex with the partner with sexual satisfaction is a difficult task to deal with. Indeed, this man also confessed that his sexual desire is something he could/would never expect to do with real women. Yuyama and Nimura (2016), who have a long experience in the media industry regarding sexuality, provide some explanation for these twisted feelings that the Japanese perception of sex, partially due to the spread of aggressive pornography, tends to lack the concept that warm emotions can be directed into sexual desire.

> When I do it alone, I can be quite cruel, depending on my own desires and interests. However, when I am with a partner, I feel a little tender thinking of that person. That kind of warm feelings and sexual desire are not compatible. With a partner, I feel somewhat relaxed or calm, and I can't continue such activities (sex) to satisfy my sexual desire.
> There is something about sexual desire that is perceived in my mind as a little bit like violence, so if I become a little calmer, the desire disappears. (071715B)

This section shed light on the priority given to masturbation among single men in Japan. Results from the focus group discussions indicate that solo sexual activity has comparative advantages over social sexual activity with a specific or non-specific partner; the former needs less time and care and is more convenient for entertaining one's sexual desire. In the next section, men's thoughts around pregnancy and reproduction are explored.

Dating Relationships and Reproductive Future with the Girlfriend

The previous section on variations of sexual partners suggested it is important for both sides (a man and a woman) to know whether they are formally dating as a girlfriend and boyfriend or just in a casual relationship. In other words, the fact of having had sex in itself is not tied to having a committed relationship, and thus, confirmation of the status by other means is expected. Omori (2021) examined the meaning of love and dating among contemporary Japanese youth and found that "dating" status is a kind of contractual relationship that binds a couple. So, a woman who is called one's girlfriend is understood to be someone special for that man with a (vague) idea of marriage in the future. Participants of the focus group sessions also shared the view that a girlfriend is different from other women with whom they simply have physical relations.

Something that newly emerged from the discussions is the reality that feelings of wanting to spend time together with a hope of sharing life as a couple, and the desire for sex, tend to be incompatible. Many participants admitted that one does not necessarily have sex with their girlfriend every time they see each other, and if they maintain the relationship for a long time, it becomes more difficult to feel the desire to have sex and the frequency of sex naturally decreases.

We used to do that (i.e., have sex) when we traveled, but not

so much anymore. I think the temperature (surrounding us) is getting to the point where it's like we enjoy being together (and that is the purpose of being together).
I think someone I want to spend time with is my girlfriend, with whom I want to go out, eat delicious food, go on trips, etc. I don't want to have sexual intercourse with that person. (071010B)

If I can fulfill my sexual desire with any person, then I can do it (have sex) with the girlfriend. But with someone I have some lasting relationship, or with someone important to me like a family member, I don't feel that way (do not feel sexual desire). (071715B)

In addition, the man in the above even stated that he has decided to intentionally separate what he looks for in a girlfriend and in a woman for physical relations. It is unknown how long and to what degree he recognizes the feeling of separation, but comments below clearly suggest his feelings. This sense of separation between love and sex has been discussed by sociologist Kaku Sechiyama (1992) in the context of the commercialization of sex. He argues that the separation of sexuality and manly love is commonly observed in the act of masturbation or the fact of having a sexual appetite by itself and it is theoretically difficult to deny the separation.

> I think to myself that the person I am dating now is not the kind of person who is looking for that much sex. If I want to satisfy my sexual desires, I can use SNS or other sexual services. So, I think I have drawn some kind of lines.
>
> (Asked if his girlfriend knows he has sexual relations with other women) I don't tell her because it's too much to ask. I tell her in various ways, for example, I can't see her because I have other plans. Well, I believe she probably doesn't know.
>
> (Clarifying whether he is hiding the fact) That's right. I don't want to be so blunt about it. So, I think I have a kind of separation between the person I enjoy my private time with and the person I enjoy my sexual time with. (071010B)

It is beyond the scope of this chapter to examine how widespread these separation feelings are among contemporary Japanese men or how they are perceived by their partners. However, this man's recognition of sexual separation and its actual practice would have significant impacts on their partners' sexual and reproductive health. From the viewpoint of women in a committed relationship with these men, women can be left being "sexless," and their sexless condition will affect their reproduction if they want a child.

On reproductive intentions, some men in the focus groups emphasized that they use contraception with their girlfriends because they want to make sure life goes as planned without an unexpected pregnancy. Because a girlfriend in a committed relationship is someone with whom they are willing to share the future, whether and when to have a child becomes a serious issue, and they are therefore watchful about the use of contraception to prevent unwanted pregnancies.

> In principle, I am not comfortable with the idea of having children before getting married. Financially at that time, it would not be good for me to have a child. My life would be restricted in many areas, and I was very concerned about that. Even now, I still worry about it a lot, so my stance is that I use contraception for sure and/or I want her to use it. (071713B)

> I always wore it (condom) in the past, and even after I got married (now divorced), I wore it when we didn't want to have children so that I could plan to have children, and when we wanted to have children, I took it off. (071713D)

In contrast to controlled and intentional reproductive behavior and associated protected sexual intercourse with a girlfriend, the opinions below imply that when sex with women in casual relationships happens, the use of contraception can be less enforced. Because men do not envision themselves as being in the position of planning a shared future with a woman in a casual relationship, more ad hoc sexual behavior can be pursued. As highlighted in the second quote, women who hold the status of the girlfriend are well protected from pregnancy, while there seems to be more room for unprotected sexual intercourse and resulting pregnancies with other women.

> It depends on the sex partner… with those whom I don't (use contraception) I just don't. It's like zero or 100. (061913A)

> I know it is not that there is no possibility of getting pregnant. So, if it (sex) happens with someone I am dating, I would definitely use contraception. (061913C)

> I think about it (the possibility of getting pregnant) when I'm calm. However, when we are doing it, or before or after, I recognize there is a possibility (of pregnancy), but I can't sometimes suppress my desire (and have sex without using a condom). (061913B)

This section discussed differences in men's reproductive intentions and the use of contraceptives. Results indicate that given the situation described here, it would be challenging to expect pregnancies from committed relationships where the frequency of sexual intercourse itself is not too active. When it does happen, men who are the main controllers of contraception by use of condoms, are more careful about using them to prevent unexpected pregnancies.

Conclusions

This chapter examined the sexual and reproductive behaviors of single men in Japan using qualitative data obtained from focus group discussions. Analyses show that having physical relations is often a first step towards a more committed and inclusive relationship. Depending on the quality of experiences together, the relationship can develop into a committed one. However, in contrast to the expectation and willingness to share life experiences, it is found that sexual activity as a shared experience in the committed relationship becomes less active. Because men feel more intimate towards women in committed relationships, they claim that sexual excitement decreases. Of course, it needs to be acknowledged that in terms of a macro viewpoint, according to the online survey results by Konishi et al. (2022a), single men who had multiple sexual partners were 12 percent (never-married) and 22 percent (other). So, we need to be careful about generalizing too much.

Besides the issue of social sexuality that requires a partner, solo sexuality, masturbation, turned out to be the dominant sexual activity among men. Akagawa (2023b) explains that there have been debates over the pros and cons of masturbation in sexual history. He argues that Western and Christian sexual ethics that treat masturbation as a taboo have come to be the "global standard" in modernity. Stories described in this chapter indeed indicate that the Japanese situation which actively and openly favors solo sexuality could be seen as an exception from the standard. However, when the disintegration of the trinity of Love-Sex-Marriage is progressing in society, it is understandable for solo sexuality to be given a significant role.

Finally, qualitative data revealed a further separation between intimacy and sex. For single men, a girlfriend is accepted to be a significant person, and because of that recognition and intimate feelings towards this specific partner, their sexual desire is described as being suppressed in a committed relationship. Although no academic data are available at present on the women's side of the story, this separation between sexual desires and intimate feelings for a specific partner will have tremendous impacts on the reproductive destiny of the couples.

Chapter 5

CONCLUSIONS

Chapter 5 CONCLUSIONS

The author started compiling this book with the hope of sharing the excitement of seeing society through the lens of demographic anthropology. The book set out to show how population dynamics and local values interact by describing two cases from Thailand and Japan. In the two cases, lowered fertility rates and ethnographic value systems closely affect each other. When a social issue is viewed from both the macro perspective and the micro (ethnographic) perspective, a much richer understanding emerges, and it is this experience of fuller understanding that this book tries to provide. Also, the book aims to present innovative data collection methods to improve the collection of quantitative and qualitative data.

Almost 20 years have passed since the original fieldwork in Bangkok was conducted. Due to the sharp fall in fertility levels, the aging of Thai society has progressed rapidly, as was demographically expected. The impacts of population aging on the lives of Thai people are now more clearly felt, and in the absence of a solid social support system, the burden on families in particular has increased. The case of Thailand shows how the concept of *bun khun* influences the achievement of co-residence, given the clear preference for co-residence with a child in old age. The analyses developed here predicted that even though the number of children per couple decreases, as long as there is a good and responsible child who recognizes and performs *bun khun*, family care of elderly and old-age co-residence can survive. With notably increasing rates of non-marriage in recent years, however, it is expected that more serious problems will occur soon when never-married people become old. Research on how this concept of *bun khun*, which has been one of the backbones of Thai social organization, will carry into a sustained low-fertility society has yet to be conducted. Also, in the context of the shrinking size of the family circle, society will have to find ways to support the old-age security of the rapidly expanding group of never-married people who don't have children.

The lack of children is also a huge issue in Japanese society. Population aging in Japan is much more advanced than in Thailand. The current book explored a possible cause of Japan's sustained low fertility from the viewpoint of expressing intimacy. This study contributed to the body of knowledge on sexlessness by examining the separation of sex and love among single Japanese men and extending the scope of the concept to solo sexuality. The analysis showed that the feeling of incompatibility between sexual desires and intimate feelings toward a specific partner contributes to a decreased frequency of sexual activity in committed relationships. A strong preference for masturbation also helps explain the absence of social sexual relations that require a partner.

Although presently there is no academic data to investigate the opinions of women left sexless in a committed relationship, this sexless situation has serious consequences for those women in terms of their sexuality and reproduction. In recent years the debate regarding the use of assisted reproductive technology has intensified in Japan. Aside from infertility caused by aging and biological/medical factors, there is also the so-called "social infertility," which arises in the relationship with a certain partner (Kugu 2021). Given the tendency of absence of sexual desires in committed relationships, let it be a marriage or dating relationship before a marriage, we can envision a new paradigm in which women who are left sexless and thus experiencing social infertility undertake activities aimed at reproduction in the form of artificial insemination.

This desexualization of reproduction can be a new possible way of having children and forming families in future Japan. Desexualization of reproduction may contribute to the improvement of reproductive health and rights of the women involved, and also as a result, will help alleviate the problems of low fertility and resulting shrinking population. Hiroshima (2020) argues that the foundation of any policy dealing with low fertility should be creating a society in which the hopes of individuals regarding marriage and children is realized. On the other hand, if people who have no such aspirations of creating a family increase in number, policies cannot work. From this point of view, as long as there is a desire to have children we may consider the scenario in which single women on their own actively pursue reproduction by bypassing romantic / sexual relationships. Of course, various legal, economic, normative, and ethical issues need to be considered before the desexualization of reproduction becomes a real issue. However, letting women conceive more independently could be a productive way of accommodating both the existing stagnation of men's sexual desires in committed relationships and the people's hope for children. The Japanese case could become an example of a forerunner for other countries that are struggling with increasing proportions of never-married people and the associated low fertility rates.

BIBLIOGRAPHY

Abe, Teruo. 2004. *Sekkusuresu no seishin igaku* [The psychiatry of sexlessness]. Tokyo: Chikumashobo. (in Japanese)

Akagawa, Manabu. 1995. "Fuufukan seikoudou no erosuka to kikakuka: 1870–1970 ni okeru kagakutekina seichishiki no keisei to henyou [The eroticization and normalization of sexual behavior in marriage]." *The Annual Review of Sociology* 8: 155–166. (in Japanese)

———. 1999. *Sekusyuariti no rekishisyakaigaku* [Historical sociology of sexuality]. Tokyo: Keiso shobo. (in Japanese)

———. 2023a. "Naze onani wa ushirometainoka [Why is masturbation a guilty pleasure?]." *Will* (June): 308–313. (in Japanese)

———. 2023b. "Onakin toiu riron: Futatsu no otokorasisa [Theory of the "onakin"(profibition of masturbation): Two types of masculinities]." *Will* (September): 310–315. (in Japanese)

———. 2024. "Sekusyuaritizu no syakaigaku no konponmondai: Gensetsu to jittai no doujitankyuu [Fundamental Issues in the Sociology of Sexualities]." In

Series. Inheritance and Development of Modern Sociology 2 Generation and Population, edited by Isamu Kaneko. Kyoto: Minervashobo. (in Japanese)

Askew, Marc. 1994. *Interpreting Bangkok: The Urban Question in Thai Studies.* Bangkok: Chulalongkorn University Press.

Ato, Makoto. 2000. *Gendai jinkougaku: Shoushi koureika shakai no kiso chishiki* [Contemporary demography: Basic knowledge on low fertility population aging society]. Tokyo: Nihon Hyouronsha. (in Japanese)

Bongaarts, John, and Robert Potter. 1983. *Fertility, Biology, and Behavior: An Analysis of the Proximate Determinants.* San Diego: Academic Press.

Chamratrithirong, Aphichat, Philip Morgan, and Ronald R. Rindfuss. 1988. "Living Arrangements and Family Formation." *Social Forces* 66(4): 926–950.

Coughlin, Richard J. 1960. *The Chinese in Modern Thailand.* Hong Kong: Hong Kong University Press.

Cowgill, Donald. 1968. "The Social Life of the Aging in Thailand." *The Gerontologist* 8(3): 159–163.

———. 1972. "The Role and Status of the Aged in Thailand." In *Aging and Modernization*, edited by Donald Cowgill and Lowell D. Holmes. New York: Appleton-Century-Crofts.

Delva, Jorge, Paula Allen-Meares, and Sandra L. Momper. 2010. *Cross-Cultural Research.* Pocket Guides to Social Work Research Methods. Oxford: Oxford University Press.

De Young, John. 1955. *Village Life in Modern Thailand.* Berkeley: University of California Press.

Fallon, Graham, and Brown Reva Berman. 2002. "Focusing on Focus Groups: Lessons from a Research Project Involving a Bangladeshi Community." *Qualitative Research* 2: 195–208.

Foster, Brian L. 1978. "Socioeconomic Consequences of Stem Family Composition in a Thai Village." *Ethnology* 17(2): 139–156.

———. 1984. "Family Structure and Generation of Thai Social Exchange Networks." In *Households: Comparative and Historical Studies of the Domestic Groups*, edited by Netting Robert, Richard R. Wilk, and Eric. J. Arnould. Berkeley: University of California Press.

Genda, Yuji, and Kawakami Atsushi. 2006. "Shugyo nikyokuka to seikodo [Divided employment and sexual behavior]." *Nihon Rodo Kenkyu Zasshi* [The Japanese Journal of Labor Studies] 556: 80–91. (in Japanese)

Goldstein-Gidoni, Ofra. 2012. *Housewives of Japan: An Ethnography of Real Lives and Consumerized Domesticity*. New York: Palgrave Macmillan.

Gubhaju, Bhakta, and Yoshie Moriki-Durand. 2003. "Fertility Transition in Asia: Past Experiences and Future Directions." *Asia-Pacific Population Journal* 18 (3): 41–68.

Guest, Philip, and Jooean Tan. 1994. *Transformation of Marriage Patterns in Thailand*. Salaya, Thailand: Institute for Population and Social Research, Mahidol University.

Hanks, Lucien. 1975. "The Thai Social Order as Entourage and Circle." In *Change and Persistence in Thai Society: Essays in Honor of Lauriston Sharp*, edited by William Skinner and A. Thomas Kirsch. Ithaca: Cornell University Press.

Heim, Franz G., Akin Rabibhadana, and Chirmsak Pinthong. 1983. *How to Work With Farmers: A Manual for Field Workers*. Khon Kaen, Thailand: Research and Development Institute, Khon Kaen University.

Hiroshima, Kiyoshi. 2020. "Sengo nihon jinkouseisakushi kara kangaeru [Thinking from the viewpoint of the history of post-war Japanese population policy]." *Japanese Journals of Health and Human Ecology* 86 (5): 231–241. (in Japanese)

Jitapunkul, Sutthichai, Napaporn Chayovan, and Jiraporn Kespichayawattana. 2002. "National Policies on Ageing and Long-term Care Provision for Older Persons in Thailand." In *Ageing and Long-term Care: National Policies in the Asia-Pacific*, edited by David R. Phillips and Alfred C. M. Chan. Singapore: Institute of Southeast Asian Studies.

Jones, Gavin W. 1993. "Consequences of Rapid Fertility Decline for Old-age Security." In *The Revolution in Asian Fertility: Dimensions, Causes, and Implications*, edited by Richard Leete and Iqbal Alam. Oxford: Clarendon Press.

———. 1998. "The Demise of Universal Marriage in East and South-East Asia." In *The Continuing Demographic Transition*, edited by Gavin. W. Jones, Robert. M. Douglas, John C. Caldwell, and Rennie M. D'souza. Oxford: Clarendon Press.

———. 2004. "Not "When to Marry" but "Whether to Marry": The Changing Context of Marriage Decisions in East and Southeast Asia." In *(Un)tying the knot: Ideal and Reality in Asian Marriage*, edited by Gavin W Jones, and

Kamalini Ramdas. Asia Research Institute, National University of Singapore.

———. 2005. "The "Flight From Marriage" in South-East and East Asia." *Journal of Comparative Family Studies* 36 (1): 93–119.

Kalton, Graham. 1988. *Introduction to Survey Sampling*. Beverly Hills: SAGE Publications, Inc.

Kamnuansilpa, Peerasit, Aphichat Chamratrithirong, and John Knodel. 1982. "Thailand's Reproductive Revolution: An Update." *International Family Planning Perspectives* 8 (2): 51–56.

Kertzer, David I., and Tom Fricke. 1997. "Toward an Anthropological Demography." In *Anthropological Demography: Toward a New Synthesis*, edited by David Kertzer and Tom Fricke. Chicago: The University of Chicago Press.

Kirsch, Thomas. 1982. "Buddhism, Sex-roles and the Thai Economy." In *Women of Southeast Asia*, edited by Penny Van Esterik. Detroit: The Cellar Book Shop.

Kitamura, Kunio. 2015. "Sei kyouiku no atarashii kadai ni tsuite kangaeru hinto wo eru: Dai 7kai danjo no seikatsu to ishikini kansuru chousa kekka kara. [Obtaining clues for thinking about new tasks of sexual education: From the findings of the 7th round of the Survey on Life and Attitude of Men and Women]." *Journal of Contemporary Study of Sexual Education* 49: 1–7. (in Japanese)

Knodel, John, Napaporn Chayovan, and Chanpen Saengtienchai. 1994. "Are Thais Deserting Their Elderly Parents?" *Bold* 4: 8–17.

Knodel, John, Chanpen Saengtienchai, and Walter Obiero. 1995. "Do Small Families Jeopardize Old Age Security? : Evidence from Thailand." *Bold* 5(4): 13–17.

Konishi, Shoko, and Emi Tamaki. 2016. "Pregnancy Intention and Contraceptive Use among Married and Unmarried Women in Japan." *Japan Health & Human Ecology* 82(3): 110–124.

Konishi, Shoko, Soyoko Sakata, Mari S. Oba, and Kathleen A. O'Connor. 2018. "Age and Time to Pregnancy for the First Child among Couples in Japan." *Jinkogaku Kenkyu [The Journal of Population Studie]* 54: 1–17.

Konishi, Shoko, Yoshie Moriki, Fumiko Kariya, and Manabu Akagawa. 2022a. "Casual Sex and Sexlessness in Japan: A Cross-sectional Study." *Sexes* 3: 254–266.

Konishi, Shoko, Yoshie Moriki, and Manabu Akagawa. 2022b. "Uebu paneru no gakuzyutsu riyou ni kansuru kousatsu [Use of internet panels in academic research]." Paper presented at the 87th Japanese Society of Health & Human Ecology, Tokyo. (in Japanese)

Kugu, Koji. 2021. *Kinmiraino <kozukuri> wo kangaeru: Funin chiryou no yukue* [Thinking about procreation in the near future: The future of fertility treatment]. Tokyo: Shunjusha Publishing Company. (in Japanese)

Lebra, Takie Sugiyama. 1984. *Japanese Women: Constraint and Fulfillment*. Honolulu: University of Hawai'i Press.

Martin, Linda G. 1988. "The Aging of Asia." *Journal of Gerontology: Social Sciences* 43(4): S99–113.

Mason, Andrew, Sang-Hyop Lee, and Gerard Russo. 2002. *As Asia's Population Ages, Worries Grow about the Future.* Asia Pacific Issues No 58. Honolulu: East-West Center.

Moriki, Yoshie. 2012. "Mothering, Co-sleeping, and Sexless Marriages: Implications for the Japanese Population Structure." *The Journal of Social Science* 74: 27–45.

———. 2017. "Physical Intimacy and Happiness in Japan: Sexless Marriages and Parent-child Co-sleeping." In *Happiness and the Good Life in Japan*, edited by Wolfram Manzenreiter and Barbara Holthus. London: Routledge.

Moriki, Yoshie, Kenji Hayashi, and Rikiya Matsukura. 2015. "Sexless Marriages in Japan: Prevalence and Reasons." In *Low Fertility and Reproductive Health in East Asia*, edited by Naohiro Ogawa and Iqubal. H. Shah. Dordrecht: Springer.

Moriki, Yoshie, and Rikiya Matsukura. 2022. "Sekkusuresu kappuru to kachikan: Syusyouryoku to sekushuariti no kanten kara [Sexless couples and family values in Japan: Analyses from fertility and sexuality viewpoints]." In *Sekusyuariti no jinkougaku* [The demography of sexuality], edited by Hiroshi Kojima and Kohei Wada. Tokyo: Harashobo. (in Japanese)

Mutchler, Jan, and Jeffrey Burr. 1991. "A Longitudinal Analysis of Household and Nonhousehold Living Arrangements in Later Life." *Demography* 28(3): 375–390.

National Institute of Population and Social Security Research. 2022. *Jinkou toukei shiryousyuu* [Demographic data collection]. (accessed September 11, 2023)

(in Japanese)

Hyou 6–12 [Table 6–12]. https://www.ipss.go.jp/syoushika/tohkei/Popular/P_Detail2022.asp?fname=T06-12.htm

Hyou 4–18 [Table 4–18]. https://www.ipss.go.jp/syoushika/tohkei/Popular/P_Detail2022.asp?fname=T04-18.htm

———. 2023. *Gendai nihon no kekkon to shussan: Dai 16kai shussei doukou kihon chousa (dokushinsha chousa narabini fufu chousa) houkokusyo)* [Marriage and child births in Japan today: The sixteenth Japanese National Fertility Survey, 2021(Results of singles and married couples survey)]. https://www.ipss.go.jp/ps-doukou/j/doukou16/JNFS16_reportALL.pdf (accessed September 11, 2023). (in Japanese)

National Statistical Office (NSO), Ministry of Digital Economy and Society. 2022. *The 2021 Survey of the Older Persons in Thailand.* https://www.nso.go.th/nsoweb/storage/survey_detail/2023/20230731135832_95369.pdf (accessed August 16, 2024).

Omori, Misa. 2021. *Gendai nihon no wakamono wa ikani "renai" shiteirunoka: Ai, sei, kekkon no kaitai to ketugou womeguru imizuke* [How the youth experience "romance" in modern Japan: Meanings surrounding the dissolution and union of love, sex, and marriage]. Kyoto: Koyo Shobo. (in Japanese)

Podhisita, Chai. 1994. "Coresidence and the Transition to Adulthood in the Rural Thai Family." In *Tradition And Change in the Asian Family*, edited by Lee-Jay Cho and Moto Yada. Hawaii: East-West Center.

Pramualratana, Anthony, Napaporn Havanon, and John Knodel. 1984.

"Exploring the Normative Basis for Age at Marriage in Thailand." In *Perspectives on the Thai Marriage*, edited by Aphichat Chamratrithirong. Salaya, Thailand: Institute for Population and Social Research, Mahidol University.

Punpuing, Sureeporn. 2023 (July). Thailand: Demographic Transition and the Aged Society. Presentation at Asia Population Association (APA) Lecture Series on National Population.

Rabibhadana, Akin. 1975. "Clientship and Class Structure in the Early Bangkok Period." In *Change and Persistence in Thai Society: Essays in Honor of Lauriston Sharp*, edited by William Skinner and A. Thomas Kirsch. Ithaca: Cornell University Press.

———. 1984. "Kinship, marriage, and the Thai social system." In *Perspectives on the Thai Marriage*, edited by Aphichat Chamratrithirong. Salaya, Thailand: Institute for Population and Social Research, Mahidol University.

Robinson, Warren, and Jawalaksana Rachapaetayakom. 1993. "The Role of Government Planning in Thailand's Fertility Decline." In *The Revolution in Asian Fertility: Dimensions, Causes, and Implications*, edited by Richard Leete and Iqbal Alam. Oxford: Clarendon Press.

Rodriguez, Katrina L., Jana L. Schwartz, Maria K. E. Lahman, and Monica R. Geist. 2011. "Culturally Responsive Focus Groups: Reframing the Research Experience to Focus on Participants." *International Journal of Qualitative Methods* 10 (4): 400–417.

Rosenfield, Allan, Anthony Bennett, Somsak Varakamin, and Donald Lauro.

1982 "Thailand's Family Planning Program: An Asian Success Story." *International Family Planning Perspectives* 8(2): 43–51.

Sato, Ryuzaburo. 2008. "Nihon no "choushoshika": Sono genin to seisaku taiou wo megutte [Ultra-low fertility in Japan: Its causes and policy responses]." *Jinko Mondai Kenkyu* 64 (2): 10–24. (in Japanese)

———. 2019. "Shoushika to sekushuariti: Nihonjin no sei koudou wa donoyouni kawattanoka [Low fertility and sexuality: How has sexual behavior of Japanese people changed]." *The Annual of the Institute of Economic Research, Chuo University* 51: 109–133. (in Japanese)

———. 2022. "Sekusyuariti ni kansuru gainen, de-ta, sihyou [Concepts, data, and indicators of sexuality]." In *Sekusyuariti no jinkougaku* [The demography of sexuality], edited by Hiroshi Kojima and Kohei Wada. Tokyo: Harashobo. (in Japanese)

Sechiyama, Kaku. 1992 "Yoriyoi sei no syouhinka he mukete [Toward better sexual commercialization]." In *Feminizumu no shuchou [Feminism's Claims]*, edited by Yumiko Ehara. Tokyo: Keiso shobo. (in Japanese)

Shand, Nancy. 1985. "Culture's Influence in Japanese and American Maternal Role Perception and Confidence." *Psychiatry* 48 (1): 52–67.

Small, Meredith. 1999. *Our Babies, Ourselves: How Biology and Culture Shape the Way We Parent*. New York: Anchor Books.

Sudman, Seymour. 1976. *Applied sampling*. New York: Academic Press, INC.

Sujatha, D Sai, and Brahmananda Reddy. 2012. "Ageing in Asia." *The Journal of International Issues* 16 (2): 114–133.

Tsuya, Noriko. 2004. "Shoushika no syakaikeizaiteki youin: Kokusaihikaku no shitenkara [Socioeconomic Factors of Declining Fertility: International Comparative Perspective]." *Gakujutsu no doukou* 9:14–18. (in Japanese)

Ueno, Chizuko. 1987. <*Watashi*> *sagashi gemu: Yokubo shimin syakai ron* [Find me game: Theory of "Yokubo shimin syakai"]. Tokyo: Chikumashobo.

United Nations, Department of Economic and Social Affairs, Population Division. 2005. *World Population Prospects: The 2004 revisions, online edition.* https://www.un.org/development/desa/pd/sites/www.un.org.development.desa.pd/files/files/documents/2020/Jan/un_2004_world_population_prospects–2004_revision_volume-i.pdf (accessed September 30, 2021).

———. 2019a. World Population Prospects 2019, online edition. Rev. 1. https://population.un.org/wpp/Download/Standard/Fertility/ https://population.un.org/wpp/Download/Standard/Mortality/ (accessed September 30, 2021).

———. 2019b. World Marriage Data 2019. Department of Economic and Social Affairs, Population Division. https://population.un.org/MarriageData/Index.html#/home (accessed August 29, 2024).

Van Esterik, Penny. 1996. "Nurturance and Reciprocity in Thai Studies." In *State Power and Culture in Thailand*, edited by E. Paul Durrenberger. CT: Yale University Southeast Asia Studies.

Williams, Lindy, Philip Guest, and Anchalee Varangrat. 2006. "Early 40s and Still Unmarried: A Continuing Trend in Thailand." *International Journal of Comparative Sociology*, 47(2): 83–116.

Wongsith, Malinee, and Siriwan Siriboon. 1999. "Household Structure and

Care of the Elderly in Thailand." In *The Family and Older Persons in China, Indonesia, and Thailand* (Asian Population Studies Series, No.152), edited by Economic and Social Commission for Asia and the Pacific. Bangkok: Economic and Social Commission for Asia and the Pacific.

Wood, James. 1994. *Dynamics of Human Reproduction: Biology, Biometry, Demography.* New York: Aldine de Gruyter.

Yuyama, Reiko, and Nimura Hitoshi. 2016. *Nihonjin wa mou sekkusu shinakunaru nokamosirenai* [Maybe the Japanese will no longer have sex]. Tokyo: Gentosha. (in Japanese)

INDEX

bun khun   15, 21, 81, 105, 109, 111, 112, 113, 118, 147, 148
casual sex   74, 125
census block   44, 45, 48–51, 84
Chinese-Thai   53, 56, 57, 59, 66, 80n1, 83n3
committed relationships   125–127, 132, 141, 142, 148–150
(use of) contraception   27, 139–142
co-residence with an aduld child   15, 59, 79, 80, 82–86, 88–90, 96–100, 102–105, 108, 117–119, 147
cultural norms   3, 39
demographic   16–20, 25, 26, 28, 65, 69, 96, 99, 117, 147
    demographic anthropology   16–18, 20, 69, 147
determinants of living arrangements   104
elderly care   85
ethical issues   17, 20, 43, 65, 68, 149
ethnographic   15, 17–19, 21, 43, 45, 60, 61, 66–69, 79, 80, 147
    ethnographic informants   60, 61
    ethnographic research   43
family of origin   111–113
focus group discussions   16, 34, 40, 72, 74, 75, 123, 124, 126, 133, 136, 142

frequency of sex   36, 37, 74, 133, 137, 141, 148
frequency of sexual intercourse   36, 37, 74, 141
friend with benefits   127, 128, 130
intimacy   15, 35, 40, 143, 148
kawanoji co-sleeping   40
living arrangements   15, 21, 28, 59, 67, 68, 79, 83, 85, 86, 101, 102, 104, 105, 108, 117
local values   19, 147
low fertility   15, 20, 25, 26, 33, 37, 119, 148, 149, 150
matching apps   129
mothering   38
never-married   25, 31, 32, 37, 38, 59, 71, 88, 91, 99, 105, 106, 111, 112, 118, 126, 142, 148, 150
    never-married children   85, 86, 88, 99, 101, 111, 112, 117–119
non-marriage   31, 32, 35, 82, 86, 118, 119, 147
old-age co-residence   15, 84, 118, 147
ordination   82, 111, 114–116, 118
patron-client relationships   63, 64
population dynamics   15, 19, 28, 147
population structures   32
pregnancy   37, 39, 136, 140, 141
reproduction   15, 17, 28, 35, 73, 86, 123, 136, 139, 148, 149
sexless couples   33, 35
sexless marriages   33, 34, 40
sexlessness   33–35, 73, 123–125, 148
sexual and reproductive behavior   21, 123, 142
sexual behaviors   36, 69, 72, 123, 124, 133

sexuality 15, 17, 35, 73, 123, 125, 135, 136, 138, 148
    social sexuality 142
    solo sexuality 21, 142, 143, 148
specific partner 74, 123, 124, 126, 136, 143, 148
total fertility rates 19, 25, 26, 32
using Zoom 17, 74, 123n1
value systems 15, 19, 147

MORIKI, Yoshie

Professor, International Christian University
Ph.D., Anthropology and Demography, Pennsylvania State University
Areas of Specialization: Demographic Anthropology, Area Studies

<Main Works>
Moriki, Yoshie. 2017. "Physical Intimacy and Happiness in Japan: Sexless Marriages and Parent-Child Co-sleeping." In *Happiness and the Good Life in Japan*, edited by Wolfram Manzenreiter and Barbara Holthus. London: Routledge.

森木美恵、米田亮太 2022.『文化横断調査：ソーシャルワーク研究のためのポケットガイド』（訳書）東京：新曜社。(Moriki, Yoshie, and Ryota Yoneda. 2022. *Cross-Cultural Research. Pocket Guides to Social Work Research Methods*. Oxford: Oxford University Press.)

森木美恵、松倉力也 2022.「セックスレス・カップルと価値観：出生力とセクシュアリティの観点から」『セクシュアリティの人口学』（小島宏、和田光平編著）東京：原書房。
(Moriki, Yoshie, and Rikiya Matsukura. 2022. "Sexless couples and family values in Japan: Analyses from Fertility and Sexuality Viewpoints." In *The Demography of Sexuality*, edited by Hiroshi Kojima and Kohei Wada. Tokyo: Harashobo.)

Low Fertility and Local Values through the Lens of Demographic Anthropology:
Living Arrangements of the Elderly in Thailand and Sexuality and Reproduction in Japan

2025 年 1 月 17 日　初版発行

著者	森木 美恵　もりきよしえ
発行者	三浦衛
発行所	春風社　*Shumpusha Publishing Co.,Ltd.*
	横浜市西区紅葉ヶ丘 53　横浜市教育会館 3 階
	〈電話〉045-261-3168　〈FAX〉045-261-3169
	〈振替〉00200-1-37524
	http://www.shumpu.com　✉ info@shumpu.com

装丁	中本那由子
写真提供	森木隆之
印刷・製本	シナノ書籍印刷株式会社

乱丁・落丁本は送料小社負担でお取り替えいたします。
©Yoshie Moriki. All Rights Reserved. Printed in Japan.
ISBN 978-4-86110-955-3 C0036 ¥4000E